THE HAIRY BIKERS'
EVERYDAY WINNERS

Si King & Dave Myers

THE HAIRY BIKERS'

EVERYDAY WINNERS

SEVEN DIALS

CONTENTS

EVERYDAY WINNERS

New and exciting ways to cook the food you love to eat!

It's been a tough couple of years and during the various lockdowns we've all been doing more cooking at home than ever before. We know a lot of people have enjoyed developing their skills in the kitchen, but money can be tight and so is time. You don't always want to spend hours coming up with something to eat, but you do want to love what you make.

We set our hearts on giving you – our readers – a cook book for every day, with a mix of easy meals and some more special recipes for when you do have a bit more time or want to give friends and family a treat. Instead of just sitting scratching our heads, we had a genius idea – we decided to find out exactly what you all like to eat. So we got on social media and asked you to tell us your five favourite go-to dinners – the ones you cook on a regular basis and that you know and love; also, your two best-loved puddings and two signature bakes. We weren't asking for recipes, that's our job. We just wanted to find out what everyone was cooking and eating. We weren't sure what sort of response we would get and we promised to list the names of 100 of the people who got in touch as a thank you – have a look at pages 284–5.

Wow – you did us proud. We were overwhelmed to find that nearly 5,000 people answered our call for help and the results were incredible. We ended up with more than 20,000 main meal suggestions, 8,000 puddings and 4,000 bakes to think about.

Top of the list were tried-and-tested dishes, such as spag bol, Sunday roasts, curries, fruit crumbles and chocolate cake – no surprises there and they are things we all love. And there were also plenty of ideas for great variations on those classics and for international, eclectic and exciting dishes that really got our taste buds going. A spreadsheet was produced and we got to work analysing all the info. Hours and hours were spent in zoom calls, coming up with recipes inspired by you that we hope everyone will want to try. We created more than 200 new recipe ideas, based on your best-loved meals, and after much discussion, we managed to whittle them down to what we think are 100 real belters for this book. It was tough but we did it!

What we wanted to do was build on your favourites. For example, people obviously love a good burger and there were loads of suggestions for exciting variations that we have worked on and developed. Big thanks to whoever suggested the Lindström burger – a Scandinavian version that includes beetroot and capers with the beef and is served with a fried egg on top. Then there's our chicken katsu burger – a fantastic fusion of eastern and western classics – and a new veggie burger. We've got some tasty new curries for you too, including a great Caribbean curry recipe and a genius combo of a rendang and a balti.

Mexican dishes, such as fajitas, have become hugely popular and we know everyone loves a fish finger, so guess what we've come up with? Fish finger fajitas! They are a joy, we promise you. And we can't wait for you to taste our margarita chicken fajitas – cocktails and supper all in one.

Then there are our new puddings and cakes. They will make you swoon. Bakewell tart meets cream and fruit to make a Bakewell trifle! The most outrageous brownies ever and a bread and butter pudding with chocolate and bananas that we're sure Elvis would have gobbled up.

One of the many things we loved about our survey was that ideas came from all corners of the world – from Bulgaria, India and Italy and everywhere in between. We're so fortunate in this country that all sorts of international ingredients are readily available in supermarkets, making it easy to eat around the world at home as well as in restaurants.

Decades ago we met a lady in Argentina who cooked us a pudding she called her 'warhorse' – a recipe she said was always successful and guaranteed to please. The aim of this book is to produce a collection of our 'warhorse' recipes – things you'll really want to eat and that you'll be happy to come back to time and time again. We hope we've got these recipes bang on and that they'll become firm favourites in your household. So, go on, dive in and maybe instead of five go-to dishes you'll end up with a hundred!

Love,

Si and Dave

A FEW LITTLE NOTES FROM US

Some useful tips for cooking success

Peel onions, garlic and other veg and fruit unless otherwise specified.

Use free-range eggs whenever possible. We reckon that 95 per cent of good cooking is good shopping - great ingredients need less fussing with - so buy the best and freshest that your budget allows.

Weigh all your ingredients and use proper measuring spoons and jugs. This is particularly important with baking recipes.

We've included a few stock recipes at the back of the book and home-made stock is great to have in your freezer. But if you don't have time, you can find some good fresh stocks in the supermarket or you can use the little stock pots or cubes.

We've given prep times and cooking times for all the recipes as guidelines but obviously prep times will vary according to your skill with a knife - and they don't include rushing out to the corner shop to get an ingredient you've forgotten! Every oven is different, so be prepared to cook dishes for a shorter or longer time, if necessary. We find a meat thermometer is a useful bit of kit to help you get perfectly cooked meat and chicken. They are easily available online and in kitchen shops.

As always, we've worked hard to make sure these recipes are easy to follow and contain ingredients that are readily available in supermarkets. For some of the spicy dishes, we've included our spice mix recipes at the back of the book for you to make if you choose. They're not difficult and they really do pack a punch of flavour, but it's fine to buy ready-made mixes if you prefer.

So get in the kitchen and start cooking. We can't wait to hear what dishes become your everyday winners.

SOUPS & SALADS

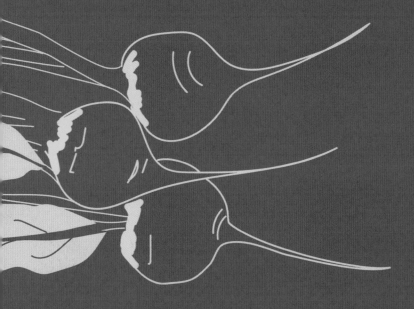

BORLOTTI BEAN SOUP

SERVES 4 | PREP: 10 MINS (PLUS SOAKING TIME} | COOK: 1¹/₂- 1³/₄ HOURS

A really good stick-to-your-ribs soup but with a nice modern touch, this is a meal in itself and it's even better on the second day. Never throw away a Parmesan rind, however dried up it might look – it adds a great boost of flavour to a soup like this. The pork element can be a ham bone, pancetta rind or prosciutto trimmings, and if you have a bone with any meat on it, chop the meat up and add it to the soup. Don't forget to soak the beans the night before.

3 tbsp olive oil

1 onion, finely chopped

1 carrot, finely diced

2 celery sticks, finely diced

4 garlic cloves, finely
  chopped

1 thyme sprig

6 sage leaves, finely chopped,
  or 1 tsp dried sage

250g borlotti beans, soaked
  overnight

1 Parmesan rind

piece of ham, pancetta
  or prosciutto

2 litres stock (ham, chicken
  or vegetable) or water

To garnish
8 sage leaves
1 tbsp butter

Heat the oil in a large saucepan and add the onion, carrot and celery. Sauté over a medium heat until softened and starting to caramelise around the edges. Add the garlic and cook for another couple of minutes, then add the thyme and sage.

Drain the borlotti beans and add them to the pan along with the Parmesan rind and ham, pancetta or prosciutto. Pour in the stock or water and bring to the boil. Allow everything to bubble quite fiercely for 10 minutes, then reduce the heat to a simmer and cook, partially covered, until the beans are tender. This will take anything from an hour to an hour and a half, depending on the age of your beans.

Remove the Parmesan rind and ham and purée the soup. Or, if you prefer, just mash half the beans to make a thick, more textured soup.

Finally, to garnish, fry the sage leaves in the butter. Top each bowl of soup with a couple of sage leaves and a drizzle of the cooking butter.

CHICKEN PHO

SERVES 4 | PREP: 20 MINS | COOK: 40 MINS

Broth

1 tsp vegetable oil

4 shallots, halved, but
   not peeled

25g root ginger, roughly
   chopped, unpeeled

4 garlic cloves, sliced

1 lemongrass stalk, chopped

4 star anise

1 cinnamon stick, broken up

1 tsp fennel seeds

4 cloves

2 bay leaves

stems from bunches of mint,
   coriander and Thai basil

2 pieces of pared lime zest

1.5 litres good chicken stock

3 or 4 chicken breasts
   (about 120g per person)

1–2 tbsp fish sauce

juice of 1 lime

1 tsp light soft brown sugar

sea salt and black pepper

Soup

4 nests of noodles

sesame oil

1 carrot, cut into matchsticks

1 red pepper, finely sliced

4 spring onions, finely sliced

100g bean sprouts

leaves from bunches of mint,
   coriander and Thai basil

Serving options

red or green chillies, sliced

sriracha or similar hot sauce

hoisin sauce

chilli oil

lime wedges

We've made this Vietnamese classic with chicken instead of the usual beef and tailored the spices accordingly. Using lean chicken breast makes this a great dish for anyone counting calories – and what it lacks in calories it more than makes up for in flavour. Don't be put off by the long list of ingredients – it's worth it. The aroma alone makes you swoon with delight.

First make the broth. Heat the oil in a large saucepan and add the shallots and ginger. Cook over a high heat until they are starting to char on the cut sides, then turn down the heat and add the garlic and lemongrass. Cook for another minute or so, stirring at regular intervals, then add all the remaining spices, herbs and the lime zest, along with plenty of salt and black pepper and the chicken stock. Season the chicken breasts and add them to the stock.

Bring to the boil, then immediately turn down the heat to a very slow simmer. Simmer gently for 10 minutes to poach the chicken, then take the pan off the heat and leave to stand for a further 10 minutes. Remove the chicken breasts from the broth and set them aside.

Return the broth to the heat and bring back to the boil. Turn the heat down and add the fish sauce, lime juice and sugar. Taste for seasoning and adjust to your liking. Leave to simmer for a further 5 minutes, then strain.

To assemble the soup, cook the noodles according to the packet instructions, then plunge them into cold water to stop them cooking. Drain and toss in a little sesame oil. Slice the chicken breasts. Divide the chicken and noodles between 4 large bowls, then add the carrot, pepper, spring onions, bean sprouts and handfuls of herbs. Taste the broth again and add more lime juice or fish sauce if necessary. Ladle the broth into the bowls and serve with your choice of chillies, sauces, chilli oil and lime wedges.

VEGGIE SCOTCH BROTH

SERVES 4 | PREP: 15 MINS (PLUS SOAKING TIME) | COOK: ABOUT 1¾ HOURS

We were filming in Scotland a while back and hit on the idea of doing a veggie version of our favourite Highland soup. This has all the ingredients of a good old-fashioned Scotch broth but without any meat. We find that with all the great vegetables, the barley and the pulses, you really don't miss the meat. The soup is still packed full of flavour and goodness and the mushroom garnish makes the perfect finishing touch. Don't forget to soak the split peas.

2 tbsp olive oil
1 large onion, finely chopped
2 celery sticks, diced
2 carrots, diced
150g swede or turnip, diced
100g celeriac, diced
    (optional)
100g pearl barley
100g split peas, soaked for
    at least 5-6 hours, then
    drained
1 tsp dried sage or fresh
    equivalent
1 thyme sprig
2 litres vegetable stock
2 leeks, sliced
½ green cabbage, shredded
sea salt and black pepper

Mushroom garnish
1 tbsp olive oil
15g butter
400g mushrooms, sliced
3 garlic cloves, crushed or
    grated
1 tarragon sprig, finely
    chopped

Heat the olive oil in a large saucepan. Add the onion, celery, carrots, swede or turnip and the celeriac, if using. Sauté over a high heat for a few minutes, just to start the softening process and get a little colour around the edges.

Stir in the barley, split peas and herbs, then pour over the stock. Season with salt and black pepper and bring to the boil. Boil for 5 minutes, then turn down the heat and simmer for about 45 minutes. Add the leeks and cabbage and simmer until the barley, split peas and vegetables are tender – this will take another 30–45 minutes.

Just before the soup is ready to serve, prepare the mushrooms. Heat the olive oil and butter in a large frying pan and add the mushrooms. Fry briskly, stirring or tossing them regularly, until well browned and tender. Add the garlic and cook for a couple of minutes longer, then season with plenty of salt and pepper and stir in the tarragon. Serve the soup garnished with the mushrooms.

SQUASH, LIME & CHILLI SOUP

SERVES 4 | PREP: 15 MINS | COOK: 30 MINS

This recipe was inspired by Mexican tortilla soup and it has a great spicy vibe. Any sort of chilli paste is fine – we like to uses chipotle for its smoky flavour and it works so well with the lime zest and juice to bring this soup to life. If you fancy, you can replace half the vegetable stock with a can of coconut milk.

2 tbsp coconut or olive oil
1 large onion, finely chopped
500g squash or pumpkin,
    peeled and diced
250g cauliflower florets,
    roughly chopped
3 garlic cloves, finely
    chopped
1–3 tsp chilli paste, to taste
zest and juice of 1 lime
800ml vegetable stock
sea salt and black pepper

To garnish (optional)
1 tsp oil
2 tbsp pumpkin seeds
½ tsp chilli paste
fresh coriander leaves

Heat the oil in a large saucepan. Add the onion and the squash or pumpkin and cook over a medium-high heat, stirring regularly, for several minutes until they start to caramelise. Add the cauliflower and garlic and cook for a few more minutes, then stir in the chilli paste and lime zest. Season well with salt and pepper. When the vegetables are well coated with the chilli paste, pour in the stock. Bring to the boil and simmer until the vegetables are completely tender – this should take about 15 minutes.

Blend the soup until smooth. Taste and add some of the lime juice – you may only need half of it to get the right balance of acidity.

For the garnish, if using, heat the oil in a small pan, add the pumpkin seeds and fry for a minute. Loosen the chilli paste with any remaining lime juice, then add it to the pumpkin seeds. Stir-fry the seeds until they look dry and roasted.

Serve the soup topped with a sprinkling of the pumpkin seeds and/or a few coriander leaves, if you like.

TORTELLINI IN BRODO

SERVES 4 | PREP: 20 MINS | COOK: 2½-3 HOURS

Brodo is Italian for broth and we both love this classic dish – basically, delicious stuffed pasta cooked in a flavourful stock. You can buy the pasta in the supermarket so this is all about the broth which does take a while to cook but is very little work. You just put it all in a pot and leave it to simmer. We've explained how to clarify the stock if you want a crystal-clear broth, but it tastes great either way. If you feel lazy, use good canned chicken consommé instead.

Broth

1kg chicken carcasses – either a mixture of raw backs/carcasses from your butcher, or a couple of leftover cooked chicken carcasses and 500g chicken wings

1 large onion, unpeeled and quartered

1 large carrot, chopped

3 celery sticks, chopped

2 bay leaves

1 large thyme sprig

1 large oregano sprig

a few parsley sprigs

a few garlic cloves

1 piece of pared lemon zest

1 tbsp peppercorns

sea salt

To clarify (optional)

2 egg whites

2 clean egg shells, crumbled

To serve

500g tortellini

Parmesan cheese, for grating

4 tbsp very finely chopped parsley

a few rasps of nutmeg (optional)

Preheat the oven to 220°C/Fan 200°C/Gas 7. Put any raw chicken carcasses and backs or chicken wings into a roasting tin with the onion and carrot. Roast for 25 minutes, then transfer to a large saucepan or stockpot with any cooked carcasses or bones. Add the celery to the pot and pour in cold water – enough to cover everything by about 3cm.

Bring to the boil and, while keeping the water at a rolling boil, watch for a mushroom-coloured foam to start collecting on the surface. Skim this off and keep skimming until the foam turns white. Add all the remaining ingredients and turn down the heat to a simmer. Leave to simmer for 2–2½ hours until the stock is a rich brown.

Strain the stock through a muslin-lined sieve. Transfer to a large container and leave to cool, then chill. Skim off the fat which will have separated out and be on top of the stock. You should find that the stock underneath has set to a jelly.

To clarify the stock, if desired, pour it into a saucepan. Whisk the egg whites and shells together to break up the whites, then stir this into the stock. Bring slowly to the boil, then simmer very gently for 15 minutes. A crust of egg, capturing any impurities in the broth, should form on top of the stock.

Break the crust and ladle the stock underneath into a muslin-lined sieve. Pour the stock back into a clean saucepan.

Season the stock with plenty of salt and bring it back to the boil. Drop in the tortellini and simmer until just cooked. Divide between 4 bowls then grate over plenty of Parmesan, sprinkle with parsley and add a rasp of nutmeg, if you like.

LENTIL SOUP

SERVES 4 | PREP: 15 MINS | COOK: 1 HOUR-1 HOUR & 20 MINS

A robust, chunky soup, this makes a good main meal with a hunk of bread and maybe a salad on the side. We like the mix of lentils here – the green or brown ones keep their shape well and add nice texture, while the red add some body to the soup. You can, of course, purée half the soup if you prefer a smoother result. The yoghurt and herb garnish adds a touch of freshness.

2 tbsp olive oil
1 onion, finely chopped
1 carrot, finely diced
½ red pepper, finely diced
1 small courgette, finely
   diced
100g green, Puy or brown
   lentils
25g red lentils, well rinsed
1–2 tsp Middle Eastern
   (baharat) spice mix (see
   p.261 or shop-bought)
   or similar
1 bay leaf
1 rosemary sprig
1.5 litres vegetable stock or
   water
sea salt and black pepper

To serve
100g thick yoghurt
1 tsp dried mint
small bunch of fresh parsley,
   finely chopped, to garnish

Heat the oil in a large saucepan. Add the onion, carrot, pepper and courgette and sauté until the onion is soft and translucent. Stir in the lentils, spice mix, bay leaf and rosemary.

Pour in the stock and bring to the boil. Boil fiercely for 10 minutes, then reduce to a simmer, partially cover the pan and cook until the lentils are tender – this will take 45–60 minutes. Season to taste and fish out the bay leaf and rosemary.

Mix the yoghurt with the mint and plenty of seasoning. Serve the soup garnished with chopped parsley and minted yoghurt.

BARLEY & BEETROOT SALAD

SERVES 4 | PREP: 15 MINS (PLUS SOAKING TIME) | COOK: ABOUT 30 MINS

Barley is great in a salad like this or you can use farro – a super-healthy grain that has a similar nutty taste to barley and is quicker to cook. Whichever grain you use, this is a big earthy salad with plenty of flavour and texture. You could add some goat's cheese, if you like.

100g barley, well rinsed
   (or farro)
1 tbsp olive oil
1 garlic clove, grated or
   crushed
150g salad leaves
200g green beans, topped,
   tailed and blanched
2 large cooked beetroots,
   peeled and diced
small bunch of dill, leaves
   only
small bunch of parsley,
   leaves only
small bunch of mint, leaves
   only
50g walnut pieces, lightly
   toasted
sea salt and black pepper

Dressing
50ml buttermilk
1 tbsp olive oil
1 tbsp lemon juice or white
   wine vinegar
½ garlic clove, crushed or
   finely chopped
1 tsp honey

Put the barley in a saucepan, cover with cold water and leave to soak for half an hour. Drain and cover with fresh water, then season with salt and bring to the boil. Simmer for about half an hour until the barley is just cooked through – you want it quite al dente. Strain, drizzle with the olive oil and add the garlic. Leave to cool to room temperature.

If you prefer to use farro instead, cook according to the packet instructions, then dress with the olive oil and garlic.

Whisk the dressing ingredients together and season with salt and pepper. Taste and adjust the seasoning or sweetness as necessary.

Arrange the salad leaves on a large platter. Add the beans and beetroots, then drizzle over some of the dressing. Sprinkle over the herbs, barley and walnuts, tossing everything very lightly so the top layers combine well. Drizzle over the remaining dressing and serve.

GOAT'S CHEESE SALAD WITH CROUTONS

SERVES 4 | PREP: 15 MINS | COOK: 15 MINS

Inspired by salads we've eaten in France, this makes a great lunch or could be served in smaller portions as a starter. Butterhead lettuce – the old-fashioned sort with lovely soft leaves and a sweet flavour – really works here and soaks up the tasty dressing nicely. It's worth making double the dressing and keeping it in a jar in the fridge for another day.

1 large butterhead lettuce, washed and roughly torn

4 slices of prosciutto, torn into strips

200g goat's cheese log, sliced

1 green apple, cored and thinly sliced (unpeeled)

fresh oregano leaves, to garnish

sea salt and black pepper

Croutons

2 thick slices of bread (about 100g), cubed

1 garlic clove, grated or crushed

2 tbsp olive oil

1 tsp mixed herbs

Dressing

3 tbsp olive oil

1 tbsp sherry vinegar

1 tsp Dijon or tarragon mustard

1 tsp honey

1 shallot, finely diced

First make the croutons. Preheat the oven to 180°C/Fan 160°C/Gas 4. Arrange the cubes of bread in a roasting tin and season with salt and pepper. Mix the garlic with the olive oil, then drizzle this over the bread and stir to make sure all the cubes are well coated. Sprinkle over the herbs. Bake for 15 minutes, stirring every 5 minutes, until the croutons are crisp and browned.

To make the dressing, whisk the olive oil, vinegar, mustard and honey together with salt and pepper. Stir in the shallot.

To assemble, put the lettuce in a salad bowl and drizzle over the dressing. Toss well, then divide the leaves between 4 plates or bowls. Add the remaining ingredients, including the croutons, and garnish with fresh oregano.

PASTA

PASTA WITH BROCCOLI & BLUE CHEESE

SERVES 4 | PREP: 10 MINS | COOK: 20 MINS

We both like a bit of blue cheese and for some reason it goes really well with broccoli. The two team up to make a nice quick pasta dish for an easy supper. Sprinkle with a little lemon zest and some chilli flakes for an extra kick and tuck in. This is full of flavour and yum factor.

2 tbsp olive oil

1 shallot, finely chopped

1 large head of broccoli,
   cut into small florets

2 garlic cloves, finely
   chopped

½ tsp chilli flakes

400g short pasta, such as
   penne

100g blue cheese, such as
   Gorgonzola or Dolcelatte,
   crumbled

sea salt and black pepper

To serve

lemon zest

chilli flakes (optional)

Heat the olive oil in a large lidded sauté pan and add the shallot and broccoli florets. Sauté over a medium-high heat until the shallot is starting to soften and brown and the broccoli is browning in patches. Add the garlic and chilli flakes and cook for a further couple of minutes, then add about 100ml of water and season with salt and pepper. Leave to steam until the broccoli is just tender.

Meanwhile, cook the pasta in plenty of boiling, salted water according to the packet instructions. When it is just al dente, reserve a couple of ladlefuls of the cooking liquid and drain the pasta.

Add the pasta to the sauté pan and stir in the blue cheese and a splash of the cooking liquid. Shake the pan until the cheese has melted – don't stir too much, as you don't want to break up all the broccoli. Add a little more of the cooking liquid until you have a creamy sauce clinging to the pasta.

Serve sprinkled with lemon zest and extra chilli flakes, if using.

LASAGNE ALLA NORMA

SERVES 6 | PREP: 20 MINS | COOK: 1-1½ HOURS

This is one for the baked pasta lovers. Spaghetti alla norma - with a sauce of aubergines and a special salted ricotta called ricotta salata - is hugely popular in Sicily and very good it is too. We've taken inspiration from this classic and created a lasagne version you're going to love. Lots of great flavours and it can all be put together in advance, ready to pop in the oven.

Tomato sauce
2 tbsp olive oil
1 onion, finely chopped
3 garlic cloves, finely
    chopped
generous pinch of cinnamon
1 tsp dried oregano
½ tsp chilli flakes (optional)
100ml red wine
2 x 400g cans of tomatoes
sea salt and black pepper

Aubergines
3 or 4 aubergines, sliced
    into ½cm rounds
50ml olive oil
1 tsp dried oregano

Ricotta filling
500g ricotta
1 egg
200g grated ricotta salata,
    or crumbled feta or 100g
    Parmesan cheese, grated
a rasp of nutmeg

To assemble
bunch of basil leaves
12 lasagne sheets
2 x 125g mozzarella balls, torn
Parmesan cheese, grated

First start the tomato sauce. Heat the olive oil in a large saucepan and add the onion. Sauté over a gentle heat until soft and translucent, then stir in the garlic and cook for another 2 minutes. Add the cinnamon, oregano, and the chilli flakes, if using, then turn up the heat and pour in the red wine. Reduce by half, then add the tomatoes. Season with salt and pepper.

Bring to the boil, then turn down the heat and cover the pan. Simmer for 10 minutes, then remove the lid and simmer gently until the sauce is reduced.

To cook the aubergines, preheat the oven to 200°C/Fan 180°C/Gas 6 and line 3 large baking trays with baking parchment. Brush the parchment with oil and arrange the aubergine rounds on the trays. Brush the aubergines with oil, then sprinkle with salt and the oregano. Roast in the oven for about 25 minutes until they have turned golden to dark brown in patches. Remove and allow to cool.

For the ricotta filling, break up the ricotta and beat in the egg until smooth. Stir in the ricotta salata, feta or Parmesan, then season with a little salt, pepper and a rasp of nutmeg.

When you are ready to assemble the lasagne, preheat the oven to 200°C/Fan 180°C/Gas 6. Take a large oven dish measuring about 30 x 20cm. Ladle a thin layer of the tomato sauce over the base and add a few torn basil leaves. Add a layer of lasagne sheets, then add more tomato sauce and more basil. Dot over spoonfuls of the ricotta mixture, then follow with a layer of aubergines. Repeat a couple of times until you have used up all the pasta, tomato sauce, aubergines and ricotta. Finish with the torn mozzarella.

Dot with a few more basil leaves and sprinkle with Parmesan. Bake in the oven for 30-35 minutes until brown and bubbling.

LOBSTER MAC 'N' CHEESE

SERVES 4-6 | PREP: 25 MINS | COOK: ABOUT 1 HOUR

Everyone loves mac 'n' cheese but in this recipe we take it to another level by adding some lobster – we used to call this dish the footballer's Saturday night special. Lobster tails can be expensive, but around Christmas in particular you can often find some real bargains on the supermarket fish counter. Otherwise, this is great made with large prawns. Totally epic.

salt
500g macaroni

Infused milk
4 lobster tails, shelled
    (shells reserved) or 400g
    large prawns, shell on
1 tbsp olive oil
100ml white wine
750ml milk
2 bay leaves
slice of onion
1 mace blade

Sauce
50g butter
1 onion, finely diced
50g bacon lardons
2 garlic cloves, finely
    chopped
1 thyme sprig
50g plain flour
1 tsp mustard powder
¼ tsp cayenne
100g Cheddar cheese, grated
100g Gruyère cheese, grated

To serve
50g fresh breadcrumbs
a few basil leaves, shredded

Preheat the oven to 200°C/Fan 180°C/Gas 6. Bring a large pan of water to the boil and salt it generously. Add the macaroni and cook it according to the packet instructions until just shy of al dente. Drain and set aside.

Separate the lobster flesh from the tails or peel the prawns and reserve the shells. Heat the oil in a saucepan and add the lobster tails or prawns. Cook them quickly on each side, then remove and set aside. Put the shells in the same pan and heat over a high heat, shaking the pan until they have taken on some colour. With the heat on high, pour in the white wine and allow it to bubble fiercely. Pour in the milk and add the bay leaves, onion and mace. Heat slowly until the milk is just below boiling point, then remove the pan from the heat. Leave to infuse until it's at room temperature, then strain the liquid into a jug and set aside.

To make the sauce, heat the butter in a large pan. Add the onion and bacon and fry until the onion is lightly caramelised and the bacon is crisp and brown. Add the garlic and thyme, then stir in the flour, mustard powder and cayenne. Stir until you have a roux (it will be lumpy because of the onion and bacon), then gradually add the infused milk mixture, stirring in between each addition, until it is all incorporated. Add 75g of each of the cheeses and stir over a low heat until the cheese has melted.

Mix the sauce with the macaroni and stir in the lobster meat or prawns. Pour into a large, shallow ovenproof dish. Mix the breadcrumbs with the remaining cheese and the basil. Sprinkle this over the macaroni. Bake in the oven for 30–35 minutes until it is piping hot, browned and bubbling.

ROAST TOMATO & TUNA LINGUINE

SERVES 4 | PREP: 10 MINS | COOK: 40 MINS

Tuna and pasta are part of everyone's early cooking experience. This recipe was inspired by a dish cooked for us by a chef in Sardinia. It's so simple and straightforward but really superb to eat. We think this will become a regular for you, as it is for us.

750g cherry tomatoes,
    on the vine
1 garlic bulb, broken into
    cloves
3 tbsp olive oil
220g can of tuna
1 tbsp capers, drained
½ tsp chilli flakes
sea salt and black pepper

To serve
400g linguine
a few basil leaves
Parmesan cheese, grated
    (optional)

Preheat the oven to 180°C/Fan 160°C/Gas 4. Arrange the cherry tomatoes in a roasting tin and sprinkle the garlic cloves around them. Drizzle with the oil and season with salt and pepper. Roast the tomatoes and garlic for 25–30 minutes until the tomatoes are soft and bursting and the garlic cloves are knife tender.

Remove the roasting tin from the oven. Discard the cherry tomato stems and squeeze the garlic flesh out of the skins. Mix the garlic and tomatoes together in the tin, then stir in the tuna, capers and chilli flakes.

Cook the linguine according to the packet instructions. Drain, reserving a ladleful of the cooking water. Add the linguine to the roasting tin and stir to combine with the sauce. Add some of the reserved cooking liquid if it seems a bit dry.

Stir through the basil leaves and serve with plenty more black pepper and some Parmesan, if you like.

TUNA PASTA BAKE

SERVES 4 | PREP: 10 MINS | COOK: 45 MINS

This is a real step up from the student/bedsit version, but at Si's insistence still contains a good helping of sweetcorn. You start by infusing the milk with flavour and then making a creamy béchamel sauce to bind the ingredients together. A really easy, comforting supper.

400g short pasta

Infused milk
750ml milk
1 bay leaf
1 mace blade
2 cloves
a few peppercorns
1 slice of onion

Sauce
30g butter
1 onion, finely chopped
30g plain flour
1 tbsp Dijon mustard
½ tsp dried oregano
2 x 150g cans of tuna, drained
250g sweetcorn kernels
100g Cheddar cheese, grated
sea salt and black pepper

First, infuse the milk. Put the milk in a small saucepan with all the aromatics and bring to the boil. Remove from the heat and leave to infuse until it has cooled to room temperature. Strain into a jug and set aside.

Cook the pasta in plenty of boiling, salted water, according to the packet instructions. Preheat the oven to 200°C/Fan 180°C/Gas 6.

To make the sauce, melt the butter in a pan. Add the onion and cook until soft and translucent. Sprinkle in the flour and stir it into the butter for a few minutes until the raw flavour has been cooked out. Gradually add the infused milk, a little a time to start with while stirring constantly in between each addition, until you have a smooth, creamy sauce around the onion. Stir in the mustard and oregano, then the tuna, sweetcorn and pasta. Season generously with salt and pepper.

Pile everything into a large ovenproof dish and sprinkle the cheese on top. Bake in the preheated oven for 25–30 minutes until the topping is nicely browned.

CHICKEN KIEV PASTA BAKE

SERVES 4 | PREP: 15 MINS | COOK: ABOUT 1 HOUR

What about this for a treat? Chicken Kiev re-imagined as a pasta bake! The chicken and pasta are bathed in a wonderful garlicky, herby, cheesy sauce, then dotted with butter and breadcrumbs for a crunchy topping and baked in the oven. Bring this to the table and see everyone's eyes light up. A great family supper.

2 large onions, cut into slim wedges

500g boneless chicken thighs (skinned if you like)

zest and juice of ½ lemon

1 tsp herbes de Provence or Italian mixed dried herbs

2–3 tbsp olive oil

300g short pasta

100g parsley, coarsely chopped

a few basil leaves

100g Parmesan cheese, coarsely grated

3 large garlic cloves, roughly chopped

30g butter

50g panko breadcrumbs

sea salt and black pepper

Preheat the oven to 200°C/Fan 180°C/Gas 6. Put the onions and chicken thighs into a large roasting tin. Sprinkle over the lemon zest and juice and the herbs. Season with salt and lots of black pepper and drizzle with the olive oil. Roast in the oven for 30 minutes, stirring every so often to keep the onions from catching. Remove from the oven and roughly slice or tear the chicken into pieces, then put them back in the tin.

Meanwhile, cook the pasta in salted water according to the packet instructions. When the pasta is al dente, drain it, reserving a couple of ladlefuls (about 200ml) of the cooking water.

Put the parsley, basil, Parmesan and garlic cloves in a food processor with salt and black pepper. Blitz to a coarse paste, then add some of the pasta water and continue to process until you have a green-flecked sauce.

Mix the sauce with the remaining pasta water. Add this and the pasta to the chicken and onion in the tin, along with 20g of the butter. Mix thoroughly. Sprinkle with the breadcrumbs and dot with the remaining butter. Bake in the oven for a further 20 minutes until the panko breadcrumbs are lightly golden and everything is piping hot.

OUR 'PROPER' BOLOGNESE

SERVES ABOUT 8 | PREP: 20 MINS | COOK: ABOUT 3½ HOURS

We all love the dish fondly known as spag bol and everyone has their own quick version. But our Bolognese sauce, also known as ragù, is the real deal, and it's well worth cooking up a big batch and stashing some in the freezer for when you're short of time. Use good stewing beef, such as shin, featherblade or even ox cheek, and check it has a nice marbling of fat. The pork mince should have some fat too - lean mince isn't right here.

750g stewing beef, in
    large chunks
2 tbsp plain flour
3 tbsp olive oil
2 onions, finely chopped
1 large carrot, finely chopped
2 celery sticks, finely
    chopped
250g pork mince
4 garlic cloves, finely
    chopped
2 tbsp tomato purée
pinch of cloves
pinch of cinnamon
2 bay leaves
1 thyme sprig
2 tsp dried oregano
leaves from 1 rosemary sprig,
    finely chopped
700ml red wine
200g puréed tomatoes
    (preferably fresh)
sea salt and black pepper

To serve
pasta, such as tagliatelle
Parmesan cheese, grated

Put the beef into a bowl and season with salt and pepper. Sprinkle over the flour and toss to coat well, then pat off any excess.

Heat a tablespoon of the oil in a frying pan. Sear the beef on all sides, making sure you allow the meat to develop a good crust. It's best to do this in batches so you don't overcrowd the pan, setting each batch aside as it is browned.

Heat the remaining oil in a large saucepan or a flameproof casserole dish. Add the onions, carrot and celery and sauté over a gentle heat until soft and translucent. You can cover the pan in between stirs to help it along if you like.

Turn up the heat and add the pork mince and garlic. Cook until the pork has browned, then stir in the tomato purée, spices and herbs.

Pour in the wine and bring to the boil. Allow it to bubble vigorously for 5 minutes, then turn the heat down to a simmer. Add the seared beef and pour in the puréed tomatoes. Season with salt and pepper.

Cover and leave to simmer for 2-3 hours, until the beef is tender. Remove the beef from the pan and gently tear it apart into much smaller pieces, then put these back in the pan. Leave to simmer, uncovered, until the sauce is well reduced. Serve with pasta and Parmesan or freeze in portions for another time.

SPAGHETTI & MEATBALLS

SERVES 4 | PREP: 30 MINS | COOK: ABOUT 1 HOUR

Who doesn't love spaghetti, tomato sauce and meatballs? We've worked hard to make sure our balls pack a punch and you're going to love the wine-infused tomato sauce. It's well worth making this with fresh tomatoes if you can.

Tomato sauce

1kg ripe tomatoes or 2 x 400g
    cans of chopped tomatoes
2 tbsp olive oil
1 onion, finely chopped
2 garlic cloves, finely
    chopped
1 tsp dried oregano
100ml white wine
pinch of sugar (optional)
handful of basil, chopped
sea salt and black pepper

Meatballs

1 tbsp olive oil
1 onion, finely chopped
2 garlic cloves, finely
    chopped
1 tsp dried oregano
zest of 1 lemon
½ tsp chilli flakes (optional)
500g pork mince
25g pine nuts, roughly
    chopped
handful of basil, finely
    chopped
75g breadcrumbs
1 egg

To serve

500g spaghetti
basil leaves, to garnish
Parmesan cheese, grated

First get the tomato sauce started. If using fresh tomatoes, peel them. To do this, core and score a cross on the base of each tomato, then plunge it into boiling water for a count of 10 (less ripe tomatoes may need a little longer). Roughly chop them or put them in a food processor and pulse. Do not strain – there's a lot of flavour in the liquid/jelly around the seeds.

Heat the oil in a large saucepan. Add the onion and sauté, stirring regularly, until it's very soft and translucent. Add the garlic to the onion and cook for another couple of minutes, then add the oregano and white wine. Allow the wine to reduce by half, then add the tomatoes (fresh or canned) and season with plenty of salt and pepper. Bring to the boil, then turn down the heat, cover the pan and simmer for half an hour. Uncover and taste. If the sauce is too acidic, add a generous pinch of sugar. Continue to simmer gently until the sauce is well reduced. Add the basil towards the end of this simmering time.

While the sauce is simmering, make the meatballs. Preheat the oven to 200°C/Fan 180°C/Gas 6 and line a baking tray with baking parchment. Heat the oil in a frying pan and add the onion. Sauté over a low heat until soft and translucent, add the garlic and cook for another minute or so. Take the pan off the heat and then add the oregano, lemon zest and chilli flakes, if using. Season well.

Put the pork mince into a bowl and add the contents of the frying pan along with the remaining ingredients. Add more seasoning and mix thoroughly until quite stiff. Divide into 20 balls and place them on the baking tray. Bake in the oven for about 15 minutes until browned and just cooked through. Add the meatballs to the sauce and let them simmer for a few minutes.

Cook the spaghetti in a large pan of water, according to the packet instructions. Spoon the meatballs and sauce over the spaghetti and garnish with basil. Serve with plenty of grated Parmesan.

RICE

SQUASH PILAF WITH BROAD BEANS & DILL

SERVES 4 | PREP: 15 MINS | COOK: ABOUT 35 MINS

A lovely veggie main, this is a new version of a pilaf we cooked in Turkey nearly 20 years ago and have always loved. We've used a Middle Eastern spice mix called baharat which you can buy in supermarkets or better still, you could make your own from our recipe on page 261.

2 tbsp olive oil

15g butter

1 onion, finely chopped

300g squash, diced

3 garlic cloves, crushed

2 bay leaves

2 tsp Middle Eastern
    baharat) spice mix (see
    p.261 or shop-bought)

1 tsp dried mint

300g basmati rice, well
    rinsed

600ml vegetable or chicken
    stock or water

200g broad beans (podded
    weight)

small bunch of dill, chopped

sea salt and black pepper

To serve
lemon wedges or sumac

Heat the olive oil and butter in a large, lidded sauté pan or a flameproof casserole dish. Add the onion and squash and sauté for several minutes until they start to soften. Add the garlic, bay leaves, spice mix and mint, season with plenty of salt and pepper, then stir to combine.

Sprinkle over the rice and pour in the stock. Bring to the boil, then turn down the heat to a simmer and cover the pan. Leave to cook for 12–15 minutes or until all the water is absorbed.

Meanwhile, prepare the broad beans. Add them to a pan of boiling water and cook for 2 minutes, then drain and refresh under cold water. Peel off the greyish skins – they should come off easily after blanching.

Sprinkle the broad beans over the rice, then cover the pan with a tea towel and a lid. Leave to steam off the heat for another 10 minutes, until the rice is dry and fluffy. Stir through the dill and serve with lemon wedges or a sprinkling of sumac.

SMOKED HADDOCK RISOTTO

SERVES 4 | PREP: 15 MINS | COOK: 30 MINS

This is definitely a risotto, not a kedgeree, and the smoked haddock works a treat. The fish can be overpowered by the curry spices in kedgeree but here it is allowed to shine. People often say no cheese with seafood, but we think a good helping of Parmesan works beautifully with the smoky flavour of the haddock.

400g smoked haddock
   (preferably undyed)
1.5 litres vegetable or fish
   stock
2 bay leaves
a few peppercorns
1 tbsp olive oil
30g butter
1 small onion, finely chopped
1 leek, sliced into rounds
2 garlic cloves, finely
   chopped
zest of 1 lemon
1 large parsley sprig, left
   whole
300g risotto rice
100ml white wine
200g peas or petits pois
   (frozen are fine), defrosted
   in hot water
50g Parmesan cheese,
   grated (optional)
sea salt and black pepper

To serve
Parmesan shavings (optional)

First, poach the haddock. Put it in a single layer in a large pan, then cover with the stock and add the bay leaves and peppercorns. Bring to the boil, then cover the pan and remove from the heat. Leave the fish to poach in the stock for 5 minutes. Remove the fish from the pan and strain the stock into a small saucepan.

As soon as the fish is cool enough to handle, flake the flesh, removing any bones or pieces of skin, and set aside.

Heat the olive oil and half the butter in a large sauté pan and add the onion and leek. Season with a pinch of salt, then cook very gently until the onion and leek are soft and becoming translucent. Add the garlic, lemon zest, parsley and rice, then stir until the rice is coated with butter and looks glossy. Reheat the stock.

Pour the wine into the pan with the rice and allow it to bubble up and evaporate away. Turn down the heat and add the stock a ladleful at a time. Keep stirring constantly until most of the liquid has been absorbed by the rice before adding more. When all the stock has been incorporated, the rice should still be slightly al dente and the creamy sauce around it should be loose enough that when you pull back your spoon along the base of the pan, the rice will slowly fall back into the trail. Add the peas.

Beat in the remaining butter and the Parmesan, if using. Carefully fold in the smoked haddock – you don't want the flakes to break up too much. Cover and leave to stand for a couple of minutes to heat through the fish, then serve with Parmesan shavings, if you like.

SEAFOOD PAELLA

SERVES 4 | PREP: 20 MINS | COOK: 35-40 MINS

We've done many a good paella recipe over the years, but we wanted to go back to a nice straightforward seafood version, using shellfish easily available from the supermarket. Make this and you'll feel like you've got a summer holiday on a plate.

2 tbsp olive oil

200g large, shelled prawns, deveined

300g cleaned squid, sliced into rounds (including the tentacles)

1 large onion, diced

3 garlic cloves, finely chopped

1 tsp fennel seeds

1 tsp hot paprika

zest of 1 lemon

leaves from a large oregano sprig, chopped

pinch of saffron, soaked in 2 tbsp water

200g fresh tomatoes, puréed

900ml fish, chicken or vegetable stock

300g paella rice

150g roast artichoke hearts (from a jar)

400g mussels, cleaned

sea salt and black pepper

To serve

parsley, chopped, to garnish

lemon wedges

Heat the olive oil in a large sauté pan or a paella pan if you have one. Add the prawns and sear them briefly on both sides until they turn pink. Remove and set them aside. Add the squid and onion and cook until the squid starts to turn golden brown.

Add the garlic, fennel seeds, paprika, lemon zest and oregano. Stir for a minute or so, then pour in the saffron and the tomatoes. Stir until the tomatoes have reduced down a bit, then pour in the stock. Season with salt and pepper.

Bring to the boil, then sprinkle in the rice in as even a layer as possible. Arrange the artichoke hearts over the rice. Leave to boil for 5 minutes, then turn down the heat and leave to simmer, uncovered, for a further 10 minutes. By this point, most of the liquid should have been absorbed by the rice.

Arrange the mussels over the rice and cover the pan. Continue to cook for about 5 minutes until the mussels are fully open – discard any that don't open. Remove the pan from the heat. Add the prawns, cover again and leave the paella to stand off the heat for a further 5 minutes.

Serve garnished with parsley and lemon wedges.

BAKED CHICKEN & MUSHROOM RISOTTO

SERVES 4 | PREP: 15 MINS | COOK: 45 MINS

Some people are happy to stand stirring a risotto for 20 minutes and find it quite relaxing. For others it's a faff, so just for you here is a splendid baked risotto that gives you all the great flavours with a lot less effort. The magic ingredient here is porcini (dried mushroom) powder. You can buy this or make your own by blitzing a little dried porcini in a spice grinder. It really does pack a punch and you'll find a little goes a long way.

1 tbsp olive oil

1 onion, very finely chopped

4 boneless, skinless chicken thighs, diced

250g chestnut mushrooms, halved

4 garlic cloves, unpeeled

1 tsp dried porcini powder

1 bay leaf

1 tsp fresh thyme leaves

300g risotto rice

100ml white wine

900ml chicken stock

sea salt and black pepper

To finish

25g butter

25g Parmesan cheese, grated, plus extra to serve

thyme leaves, to garnish

Preheat the oven to 200°C/Fan 180°C/Gas 6.

Heat the oil in a large flameproof casserole dish. Add the onion, chicken and mushrooms and sauté quickly until the chicken is lightly browned. Add the garlic cloves, sprinkle in the porcini powder and stir.

Add the herbs, risotto rice, wine and chicken stock. Season with salt and pepper. Put a lid on the pan or cover tightly with foil. Bake in the oven for 20 minutes, then remove, stir and return to the oven for a further 15 minutes or until the rice is cooked and surrounded by a creamy sauce – it may need up to another 5 minutes.

Remove from the oven and beat in the butter and Parmesan. Garnish with a few thyme leaves and serve with more Parmesan to add at the table.

CHICKEN & CHORIZO PAELLA

SERVES 6-8 | PREP: 20 MINS | COOK: ABOUT 40 MINS

This is a keeper if you love your paella but you're not keen on seafood. It's packed full of juicy chicken thighs, fiery chorizo and veggies and it tastes bang on. It's a one pot too, so not a drop of flavour goes to waste. We know some people don't reckon on including chorizo in paella but we like it.

1 tbsp olive oil

150g cooking chorizo, sliced
   into rounds

1 large onion, finely chopped

1 red pepper, diced

4 garlic cloves, finely
   chopped

1 tsp dried oregano, or 1 tbsp
   fresh oregano, chopped

2 bay leaves

zest and juice of 1 lemon

500g boneless, skinless
   chicken thighs, diced

1 tbsp tomato purée

100ml white wine

large pinch of saffron
   strands, ground with
   ½ tsp sea salt

1.25 litres chicken or
   vegetable stock

500g paella rice

100g broad beans or peas

100g runner beans, shredded

sea salt and black pepper

To serve
lemon wedges
parsley, finely chopped

Heat the olive oil in a large paella pan or sauté pan and add the chorizo. Brown quickly on all sides until plenty of the orange fat has rendered out, then remove the chorizo with a slotted spoon and leave it to drain on some kitchen paper.

Add the onion and pepper to the pan and sauté over a low heat until the onion is soft and translucent. Add the garlic, oregano, bay leaves and lemon zest and give it a quick stir before adding the chicken and the tomato purée. Stir until the chicken is well coated with the oil and purée.

Turn up the heat and pour in the wine. Let it evaporate away, then sprinkle in the saffron. Pour in the stock and bring to the boil. Season with salt and pepper, then sprinkle in the rice, in as even a layer as possible, followed by the broad beans or peas and the runner beans. Make sure that the chicken and veg are spread around the pan evenly, as you should not stir the paella after this point. Sprinkle over the lemon juice and the chorizo.

Bring back to the boil and cook for 5 minutes, then turn down the heat and leave to simmer gently until the rice is just al dente. Remove from the heat, cover with a tea towel and a lid if possible, then leave to stand for 10 minutes.

Serve with lemon wedges and a sprinkling of finely chopped parsley.

SAUSAGE & FENNEL RISOTTO

SERVES 4 | PREP: 15 MINS | COOK: 35-40 MINS

One of our favourite risottos, this is a good hearty supper with plenty of Italian pizazz from the lemon zest and vermouth – classic flavours with a touch of finesse. Great if you can get fennel sausages, but we add some fennel seeds to the rice so they're not essential. We just know you're going to love this dish.

2 tbsp olive oil

4 sausages, skinned and
  broken up

30g butter

1 fennel bulb, finely chopped,
  any fronds reserved

3 garlic cloves, finely
  chopped

2 pieces of pared lemon zest

1 tsp fennel seeds

300g risotto rice

100ml white wine or
  vermouth

1 litre chicken stock, warmed
  through

50g Parmesan cheese,
  grated

sea salt and black pepper

To serve

parsley and fennel fronds,
  finely chopped

Heat a tablespoon of the oil in a frying pan and add the sausages. Fry for 3-4 minutes without stirring, until they have developed a brown crust, then break them up further with a wooden spoon and stir. Keep cooking until the sausages are browned all over and cooked through, but still juicy. Drain on some kitchen paper and set aside.

To make the risotto, heat the rest of the oil and half the butter in a large sauté pan or a clean frying pan. Add the fennel and cook over quite a high heat until it is softening and starting to caramelise. Stir in the garlic, lemon zest and fennel seeds and cook for another 2 minutes. Add the rice and stir until it is glossy with butter. Season with salt and pepper.

Pour in the wine or vermouth and bring to the boil. When the wine has almost completely boiled off, start adding the stock a ladleful at a time. Stir the stock into the rice over a medium heat and keep stirring until most of it has been absorbed by the rice. Repeat until you have used all the stock – it should take at least 20 minutes. By this point the rice will still be slightly al dente and suspended in a creamy sauce.

Beat in the rest of the butter and half the Parmesan and check the consistency of the rice – you should be able to make a clear path on the base of the pan with your spoon, but the rice should slowly fall back behind it.

Remove the lemon zest and stir in the sausage. Leave to stand for a couple of minutes to warm the sausage through, then sprinkle with parsley and fennel fronds. Serve with more grated Parmesan.

KEEMA RICE

SERVES 4 | PREP: 10 MINS | COOK: 40 MINS

A sort of cross between a pilaf, fried rice and a mince curry, this makes a really tasty, hassle-free midweek supper. And it's a one pot, so saves on washing up. Just be sure to allow time for the steaming at the end which allows all the flavours to blend beautifully.

1 tbsp coconut oil
1 onion, diced
200g minced lamb
15g root ginger, grated
3 garlic cloves, finely
    chopped
small bunch of coriander,
    finely chopped
1 tbsp curry powder
1 tbsp tomato purée
300g peas
200g basmati rice, rinsed
sea salt and black pepper

To serve (optional)
green chillies
yoghurt

Heat the oil in a large, lidded saucepan or a flameproof casserole dish. Add the onion and sauté until golden brown, then turn up the heat and add the lamb. Cook, stirring regularly, until the lamb is nicely browned and cooked through.

Add the ginger, garlic, half the coriander and the curry powder. Continue to cook, stirring constantly, until everything is well coated in the curry powder, then add the tomato purée and continue to stir for another few minutes until the mixture is quite dry.

Pour in the peas and rice, along with 400ml of water. Season with salt and pepper, then bring to the boil. Cover and turn the heat down to a simmer. Leave to cook for 12–15 minutes until the liquid has been absorbed and the rice is just cooked.

Remove the pan from the heat and cover with a tea towel and the lid. Leave to steam for another 10 minutes, then serve with the rest of the coriander and the green chillies and yoghurt, if using.

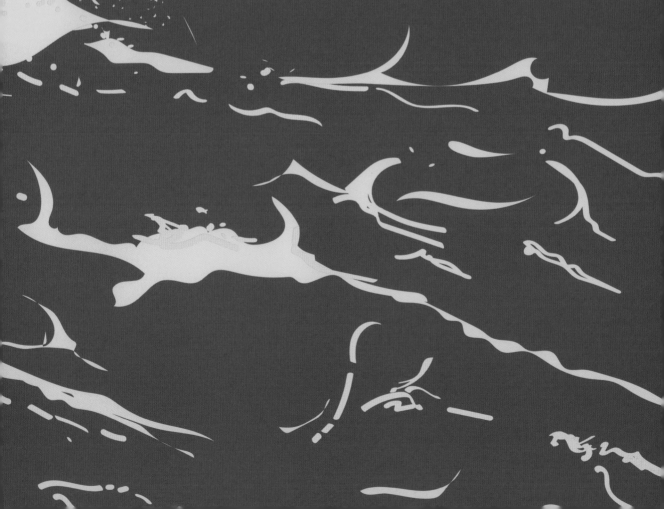

SEAFOOD

SRI LANKAN FISH CURRY

SERVES 4 | PREP: 25 MINS | COOK: 30-40 MINS

Marinade

juice of 1 lime
½ tsp ground turmeric
½ tsp chilli powder
300g firm white fish, such
    as cod or haddock, cut
    into chunks
400g pack frozen seafood
    mix
sea salt and black pepper

Paste

15g root ginger, chopped
4 garlic cloves, chopped
3 bird's-eye chillies, finely
    chopped

Curry

1 tbsp coconut oil
1 large onion, finely sliced
1 tsp mustard seeds
1 tsp fennel seeds
12 curry leaves
1 tsp ground coriander
½ tsp ground fenugreek
½ tsp ground cardamom
200g fresh tomatoes, puréed
2 tbsp tamarind purée
400g can of coconut milk

To serve

1 tsp coconut oil
a few curry leaves
a few coriander sprigs
lime wedges
basmati rice (see p.262)

Yes, there are lots of spices in this but they add so much flavour. Once you've got them organised, this is a quick curry to cook and you can use one of those packs of frozen seafood mix from the supermarket which are perfect for this recipe. Just take care not to break the fish up too much when you stir it into the curry. This makes a fabulous feast and it's good served with some rice to soak up the tasty juices.

First marinate the fish and seafood. Put the lime juice in a bowl with the turmeric, chilli powder and plenty of seasoning. Stir to combine, then add the fish and the seafood mix (no need to defrost) and toss until it is all covered with the spices. Set aside while you make the paste and curry.

To make the paste, put the ginger, garlic and chillies into a small food processor with a tablespoon of water and blitz to a fairly smooth paste.

Heat the coconut oil in a large saucepan or a flameproof casserole dish. Add the onion and cook over a medium heat until it's soft and translucent. Turn up the heat and add the mustard and fennel seeds and the curry leaves. When the curry leaves crackle, add the paste and the spices and stir for 2-3 minutes.

Add the tomatoes, tamarind and coconut milk to the pan, along with 200ml of water. Season with salt and pepper. Bring to the boil, then turn down the heat and simmer, covered, for 15 minutes, or until the raw flavour of the tomatoes has been cooked out. Remove the lid and simmer for another few minutes to reduce the sauce.

Add the fish and seafood to the pan. Leave to simmer over a low heat for a few minutes until the fish is completely cooked through.

To serve, heat the coconut oil in a frying pan and add the curry leaves. When they start to crackle, remove them from the heat. Garnish the curry with the leaves, coriander sprigs and serve with lime wedges and rice.

PRAWN, KALE & COCONUT STIR-FRY

SERVES 4 | PREP: 20 MINS | COOK: 15 MINS

Prawns
180–200g raw peeled prawns
zest of 1 lime
pinch of chilli flakes
sea salt and black pepper

Stir-fry
1–2 tbsp coconut or
   vegetable oil
2 lemongrass stems, white
   core only, finely chopped
1 shallot, finely sliced
1–2 bird's-eye chillies,
   deseeded, finely chopped
50g fresh coconut, thinly
   sliced
15g root ginger, cut into
   matchsticks
3 garlic cloves, sliced
1 large carrot, cut into
   matchsticks
½ red pepper, cut into thin
   strips
150g kale, leaves stripped
   from stems and roughly
   torn
2 tbsp Thai fish sauce, plus
   extra if needed
juice of 1 lime

To serve
2 nests of noodles, cooked
   according to packet
   instructions
sesame oil
a few mint leaves

There's some prep to get done here but the actual cooking takes no time. Best thing is to do what we do on our TV shows – get everything chopped and ready in little bowls, then go for it. Dinner will be on the table in minutes and proper tasty it is too. You could use cavolo nero instead of kale, if you prefer.

Put the prawns in a bowl and season them with salt, then toss in the lime zest and chilli flakes. Leave to marinate while you get everything else prepared before you start stir-frying.

When you are ready, heat half the oil in a large wok. When the air above the oil is starting to shimmer, throw in the prawns and stir-fry very quickly until they are pink and opaque. Remove from the wok and set aside.

If there is very little oil left in the wok, add more. When the air is shimmering again, add the lemongrass, shallot, chillies, coconut, ginger and garlic, then the carrot and red pepper. Stir-fry for 2–3 minutes, then add the kale. Stir-fry for a further couple of minutes, then pour in the fish sauce and lime juice. Keep cooking until the kale has wilted down – it will keep some texture however long you cook it for.

Put the prawns back in the wok along with the cooked noodles and heat through. Taste for seasoning and add salt and pepper and more fish sauce, if you like. Drizzle with sesame oil and add a few mint leaves before serving.

FISH & CHORIZO TRAY BAKE

SERVES 4 | PREP: 15 MINS | COOK: 50 MINS

A long while back, we cooked chorizo-coated fish on a beach in Patagonia for one of our television programmes. We loved the recipe and we've made it lots over the years. Now, we've adapted it and added veg to make a tasty tray bake that's full of colour and flavour.

2 red onions, cut into wedges

2 red peppers, cut into thick slices

2 large courgettes, cut into chunks

2 tbsp olive oil

zest of 1 lemon

3 thyme sprigs

100ml red wine

2 x 400g cans of butter beans

250g cherry tomatoes

sea salt and black pepper

Fish and crust

100g chorizo, skinned and sliced

100g breadcrumbs

1 garlic clove, finely chopped

a few basil leaves

4 x fairly thick fillets of white fish, such as cod, haddock or hake, skinned

Preheat the oven to 200°C/Fan 180°C/Gas 6. Arrange the onions, peppers and courgettes in a roasting tin and drizzle over the olive oil. Sprinkle the lemon zest over the veg and mix thoroughly. Add the thyme sprigs to the tin and season with salt and pepper, then roast in the oven for 20 minutes. Pour in the red wine and add the butter beans, then return to the oven for a further 10 minutes.

Meanwhile, make the crust. Put the chorizo in a dry frying pan and fry until crisp and much of the fat has rendered out. Drain on kitchen paper. When cool, put the chorizo in a food processor with the breadcrumbs, garlic and basil leaves. Blitz until the mixture is finely textured with a paste-like quality. Season the fish fillets, then press some chorizo mixture on top of each one.

Add the fish fillets to the roasting tin and dot the cherry tomatoes around them . Put the tin in the oven for a further 15 minutes until the fish is cooked through.

MEDITERRANEAN FISH PIE

SERVES 4 | PREP: 20 MINS (PLUS CHILLING TIME) | COOK: ABOUT 1 HOUR & 20 MINS

Fish pie doesn't always have to be topped with mash. This recipe was inspired by spicy fish empanadas and is a real treat. There are a few important things to note. First, the fish must be cooked before putting it in the pie or it will make the sauce watery. Second, make sure the pie is well chilled before it goes in the oven or the fish will be overcooked by the time the pastry is done. And lastly, we think it tastes much better made with ripe fresh tomatoes rather than canned. Trust us on all this and you're on to a winner.

1 tbsp olive oil

15g butter

3 leeks, cut into rounds

1 large fennel bulb, diced

2 garlic cloves, finely chopped

1 tbsp plain flour

large pinch of saffron, soaked in 2 tbsp warm water

1 tsp fennel seeds

1 tsp finely grated orange zest

100ml white wine

150ml fish stock or water

200g fresh, ripe tomatoes, puréed

500g white fish, diced

100g shelled raw prawns

100g cleaned scallops (or another 100g prawns)

sea salt and black pepper

Crust

flour, for dusting

200g puff pastry

1 egg, beaten with 1 tbsp water

Heat the oil and butter in a large lidded sauté pan and add the leeks, fennel and garlic. Stir until nicely coated in the oil and butter, put the lid on the pan, then leave to cook gently until tender – this will take up to 10 minutes.

Stir in the flour for a couple of minutes, trying not to break up the leek rounds too much, then add the saffron, fennel seeds and orange zest. Stir again, then pour in the white wine. Bring to the boil, then add the stock or water and the tomatoes. Season with salt and pepper.

Bring to the boil again, stirring constantly, then turn down the heat and simmer until the sauce has reduced and has the consistency of thick double cream. Add the fish, cover and leave to poach for 3–4 minutes. Add the prawns and scallops, cover again and cook for 2–3 minutes until they are just cooked through.

Transfer the mixture to a pie dish and cover. Leave to cool, then put it in the fridge until well chilled. You can save time, if you like, by putting the dish in the freezer for half an hour. This stage is important – the fish has to be very well chilled so it doesn't overcook while the pastry is browning.

Preheat the oven to 200°C/Fan 180°C/Gas 6. Dust a work surface with flour and roll out the pastry to a size that will fit your pie dish.

Remove the pie from the fridge or freezer and brush the pie dish rim with water. Lay the rolled-out pastry over the filling. Brush the pastry with beaten egg and make a couple of incisions to release the steam.

Place on a baking tray and bake in the preheated oven for 30–40 minutes until the pastry is puffed up and golden brown and the filling is piping hot.

SMOKED MACKEREL GRATIN

SERVES 4 | PREP: 20 MINS | COOK: 1 HOUR & 20 MINS

Smoked mackerel is cheap, plentiful and very tasty, and it's readily available, even in the small supermarkets. The gherkins and horseradish really compliment the robust smokiness of the fish and help make a gratin to be proud of. By the way, here's a useful tip - we find that adding a teaspoon of flour to gratins like this helps prevent the milk and cream from separating.

butter, for greasing and dotting on top
500g floury potatoes, thinly sliced (preferably with a mandolin)
250g celeriac, peeled and thinly sliced
2 leeks, sliced into thin rounds
200g smoked mackerel fillets, skinned and broken up
2 tbsp horseradish sauce
3 tbsp finely chopped gherkins or cornichons
200ml double cream
100ml whole milk
1 tsp plain flour
sea salt and black pepper

Preheat the oven to 200°C/Fan 180°C/Gas 6. Generously butter a shallow ovenproof dish.

Bring a large pan of water to the boil. Add plenty of salt, then drop in the potatoes. Simmer for 3 minutes, then add the celeriac and leeks. Simmer for a further 2 minutes, then drain.

To layer the gratin, start with a single layer of potatoes, followed by the celeriac, leeks and smoked mackerel. Dot over some horseradish and chopped gherkins or cornichons and season with salt and pepper as you go. Repeat until you have used up all the ingredients, making sure you finish with a layer of potatoes.

Mix the cream, milk and flour together, whisking lightly to make sure they are well combined. Season with more salt and pepper, then pour over the gratin. Press the vegetables down so the cream just covers them. Dot the top with butter.

Cover with foil and bake in the oven for 40 minutes. Remove the foil and bake for a further 25-30 minutes until the vegetables are tender and the top is lightly browned. Leave to stand for a few minutes before serving.

FISH FINGER FAJITAS

SERVES 4 | PREP: 15 MINS | COOK: 30 MINS

Guys – this is seriously brilliant and takes the fish finger sandwich to a totally new level. The fish fingers, pepper and onion with the wonderful jalapeño sauce, all wrapped up in tortillas, taste like they were always meant to be together. Captain Birdseye meets Pablo Escobar – it's our biggest triumph yet.

16 fish fingers
2 tbsp olive oil
1 large red onion, finely sliced
1 red pepper, finely sliced
3 garlic cloves
1 tsp ground cumin
1 tsp chipotle paste
zest and juice of 1 lime

Jalapeño sauce
150g mayonnaise
50g soured cream
2 fresh green jalapeños,
    finely chopped
1 tbsp pickled jalapeños,
    finely chopped
2 tbsp finely chopped
    coriander stems
2 cornichons, finely chopped
zest and juice of 1 lime
½ tsp sugar
sea salt and black pepper

To serve
warm tortillas
100g Cheddar cheese, grated
extra pickled jalapeños
fresh coriander leaves
lime wedges

First make the jalapeño sauce. Put all the ingredients in a bowl with a teaspoon of salt and plenty of black pepper. Mix thoroughly and leave to stand so the flavours can develop – the lime juice will loosen up the mayonnaise a lot.

Cook the fish fingers in the oven according to the packet instructions.

Meanwhile, heat the olive oil in a large frying pan and add the onion and red pepper. Cook over a medium-high heat until they start to brown around the edges but still have a firm texture. Add the garlic, cumin and chipotle paste, followed by the lime zest and juice. Stir and continue cooking for a few more minutes, just to let the vegetables soften a little more. Remove the fish fingers from the oven and roughly break them up. Add them to the pan and gently toss everything together.

Pile the fish fingers and vegetables on to warm tortillas and dress with the jalapeño sauce. Sprinkle with any of the garnishes and squeeze over some lime juice before eating.

SPICY FISH & CHIPS

SERVES 4 | PREP: 15 MINS | COOK: 45 MINS

We all enjoy a Friday night treat from the local chippy, but proper fish and chips can be quite a business to make at home. Instead, try our super-easy version with everything cooked in the oven. Both the fish and potatoes have great spicy flavours and we serve this with a chilli-flavoured pea purée – fish, chips and mushy peas with a touch of Biker magic.

4 skinless fillets of white fish, such as cod or haddock, cut in half lengthways
1 tbsp plain flour
½ tsp turmeric
½ tsp ground cardamom
½ tsp curry powder
½ tsp chilli powder
1 egg, beaten
100g panko breadcrumbs
olive oil, for drizzling
sea salt and black pepper

Potatoes
500g potatoes, left unpeeled and cut into small chunks
2 tbsp olive or vegetable oil
2 tsp cumin seeds
2 green chillies, finely chopped

Pea and coriander purée
400g peas (frozen are fine)
small bunch of coriander
2 tbsp crème fraiche
1 tbsp lime juice
pinch of chilli powder

First start the potatoes. Preheat the oven to 200°C/Fan 180°C/Gas 6. Bring a large pan of water to the boil and add salt. Add the potatoes and cook for 4–5 minutes, then drain. Pour the oil into a roasting tin and add the potatoes. Toss and sprinkle in the cumin seeds, then roast in the oven for 25 minutes.

Pat the fish fillets dry. Mix the plain flour with the spices, salt and pepper. Dip the fish into the seasoned flour and coat well. Pat off any excess, then dip the fish in the beaten egg and lastly into the panko breadcrumbs.

Remove the potatoes from the oven and sprinkle with the green chillies, then lay the fish on top. (If the tin seems too crowded, cook the fish in a separate tin instead.) Drizzle with a little olive oil and cook for a further 10 minutes. Remove from the oven.

Simmer the peas in hot water for 2–3 minutes. Drain and purée with the coriander, crème fraiche, lime juice and chilli powder. You can make this as coarse or as smooth as you like. Warm through again and serve with the fish and potatoes.

SALMON EN PAPILLOTE

SERVES 4 | PREP: 15 MINS | COOK: 30 MINS

Our survey of your favourite dishes showed that salmon is a hugely popular fish and this is a great way of cooking it. En papillote is a fancy way of saying 'in paper' and that's what this is – more of a one-bag wonder than a one-pot wonder. The citrusy, buttery juices make enough of a sauce and everyone gets their own parcel of joy. If you don't have baking parchment you could use foil, but it doesn't look as pretty.

500g new potatoes, thickly
   sliced
a few mint sprigs
butter, for greasing and
   dotting on top
2 small courgettes, thinly
   sliced
200g slim green beans,
   trimmed
4 thick salmon fillets or
   steaks (preferably wild)
a few tarragon sprigs
1 lemon, thinly sliced
2 tbsp capers
100ml white wine
sea salt and black pepper

Preheat the oven to 200°C/Fan 180°C/Gas 6.

Bring a pan of water to the boil and add plenty of salt. Add the potatoes and half the mint sprigs and cook until the potatoes are just tender. Drain thoroughly.

Cut out 4 squares of baking parchment (roughly 30 x 30cm) and butter them generously. Divide the potatoes between the 4 pieces of parchment and dot with more butter. Arrange the courgettes and beans over the potatoes and season with salt and pepper.

Season the pieces of salmon and place them on top of the vegetables. Add the remaining mint, along with the tarragon, lemon slices and capers. Pour over the white wine, dividing it between the parcels.

Bring up 2 sides of each parchment piece and fold into a pleat. Scrunch the ends together. Place the parcels on a baking tray or tin and place them in the oven.

Bake for 15 minutes, then remove the tray from the oven. Give everyone a parcel so they can open them at the table and enjoy the fabulous aromas.

MUSSELS WITH BACON, CIDER & CREAM

SERVES 4 | PREP: 15 MINS | COOK: 25 MINS

Mussels are cheap and make a quick, tasty supper. In this recipe, we partner them with bacon, cider and a touch of mustard and also throw in some new potatoes to make the dish more substantial. If you prefer, though, you could leave out the potatoes and serve the mussels with crusty bread to mop up the juices. Or you could have both!

2kg mussels
2 tbsp olive oil
2 shallots, finely chopped
100g bacon lardons
300g baby new potatoes, scrubbed
300ml cider
2 tarragon sprigs
1 parsley sprig
2 tsp Dijon mustard
100ml double cream or crème fraiche (optional)
sea salt and black pepper

To serve
tarragon sprigs, finely chopped

First prepare the mussels. Discard any that are open and refuse to tightly close when sharply tapped. Pull off the beards and wash the mussels thoroughly under cold running water.

Heat the oil in a large, flameproof casserole dish or a saucepan with a lid. Add the shallots, bacon and potatoes. Fry, stirring regularly, until both are crisp and brown. Pour in the cider and add the herbs, then whisk in the mustard. Season with salt and pepper. Bring to the boil, then put the lid on, turn down the heat and simmer for about 10 minutes, until the potatoes are tender.

Turn up the heat again and add the mussels to the pan. Cover and cook the mussels for 3-4 minutes, shaking the pan from time to time and checking them until they are fully opened. Discard any mussels that remain closed.

Pour in the cream or crème fraiche, if using, and leave to simmer for another couple of minutes. Serve with a sprinkling of finely chopped tarragon.

CHICKEN & DUCK

CHICKEN HANDI

SERVES 4 | PREP: 20 MINS | COOK: ABOUT 45 MINS

A brilliant everyday chicken curry, chicken handi is a sort of Pakistani version of a balti. It has a rich tomato/yoghurt base like tikka masala, so ticks all the boxes for satisfying our curry cravings. The spicing is perfect but you could use two tablespoons of medium curry powder instead if you prefer. You could say that we think this recipe will come in very handy!

600g skinless, boneless
   chicken thighs or thighs
   and breast, diced
juice of ½ lemon
2 tbsp oil or ghee
2 onions, finely sliced
4 garlic cloves, crushed
15g root ginger, grated
1 tbsp cumin seeds
1 tbsp ground coriander
1–2 tsp chilli powder
1 tsp ground turmeric
1 tsp ground fenugreek
½ tsp cinnamon
400g can of chopped
   tomatoes
150ml Greek-style yoghurt
1 tsp garam masala
sea salt and black pepper

To serve
fresh coriander leaves
green chillies, finely chopped
   or sliced
long-grain or basmati rice
   (see p.262)
lemon wedges

Season the chicken with salt and pepper and toss it in the lemon juice. Set it aside to marinate while you make the sauce for the curry.

Heat the oil or ghee in a large flameproof casserole dish. Add the onions and cook over a medium-high heat until golden brown. Add the garlic and ginger and fry for a few minutes longer, then add the spices. Continue to cook for a couple more minutes, then add the tomatoes and 200ml of water.

Bring to the boil, then turn down the heat and leave to simmer, covered, for about 10 minutes to allow the flavours to develop. Add the chicken and stir to coat it in the curry sauce. Cook for another 10 minutes until the chicken is cooked through, then check the seasoning. Stir in the yoghurt and garam masala and continue to cook very gently until the sauce has reduced further and you start seeing red oil collecting on top of the curry.

Sprinkle with coriander and green chillies and serve with rice and some lemon wedges for squeezing over.

CHICKEN, CASHEW & PINEAPPLE STIR-FRY

SERVES 4 | PREP: 20 MINS (PLUS MARINATING TIME) | COOK: ABOUT 15 MINS

Chicken
200g skinless, boneless
    chicken breast or thigh
    meat, finely sliced
1 tbsp soy sauce
1 tbsp mirin
1 tsp oil
2 tsp cornflour

Sauce
1 tbsp soy sauce
1 tbsp mirin
1 tsp rice wine vinegar
1 tbsp pineapple juice

Stir-fry
2 tbsp oil
2 shallots, finely sliced
½ red pepper, diced
100g mangetout
50g baby corn
1 hot red chilli, finely
    chopped, or ½ tsp hot
    chilli flakes
10g root ginger, cut into
    matchsticks
2 garlic cloves, finely
    chopped
35g cashew nuts
100g diced pineapple
    (canned or fresh)

To serve
sesame oil
fresh coriander, chopped

This is proper cooking – a great fusion dish and a tasty way to get some of your five a day! Marinating chicken in this way is called velveting and makes it beautifully soft and tender, so is well worth doing. Velveting also works well with pork loin.

Put the chicken in a bowl and pour over the soy sauce and mirin. Leave it to marinate for 10 minutes, then stir in the oil followed by the cornflour. Make sure the chicken is completely coated and there are no white streaks of cornflour.

Mix the ingredients for the sauce together and set aside.

Heat half the oil in your wok. When the air is shimmering above the oil, add the chicken and stir fry for 2–3 minutes until it is coloured on all sides and just cooked through. Remove the chicken from the wok, place it in a clean bowl, then set aside.

Wipe out the wok and add the remaining oil. Add the shallots, red pepper, mangetout and corn and stir-fry for 3–4 minutes, then add the chilli, ginger, garlic and cashew nuts. Continue to stir-fry until the cashews have taken on some colour.

Stir in the pineapple and chicken, then pour over the sauce. Continue to cook over a high heat until the chicken is heated through and the vegetables are just al dente. Garnish with a drizzle of sesame oil and some chopped coriander.

POT-ROAST CHICKEN WITH PASTA

SERVES 4 | PREP: 15 MINS | COOK: ABOUT 1 HOUR & 30 MINS

We all love a Sunday roast and this is just as delicious as the traditional way but even easier, as the chicken and gravy are all in one pot. There's a bit of a Mediterranean vibe to this recipe with the olives and the tomatoes that cook down into a lovely soft mixture. Great served with the tagliatelle but also good with roasties.

2 tbsp olive oil

1 oven-ready chicken

2 red onions, cut into wedges

1 garlic bulb, divided into
  cloves

a few rosemary sprigs

2 pieces of pared lemon zest

100ml white wine or
  vermouth

600g fresh, ripe but firm
  tomatoes

50g olives

sea salt and black pepper

To serve

400g tagliatelle

a few basil leaves, to garnish

Preheat the oven to 180°C/Fan 160°C/Gas 4.

Heat the oil in an ovenproof casserole dish large enough to hold the chicken. Season the chicken with salt and brown it, breast-side down. Remove, then add the onions and cook them over a high heat until they are taking on some colour.

Place the chicken back in the dish, breast-side up. Put a few garlic cloves, a sprig of rosemary and a piece of lemon zest in the cavity of the chicken and add the rest to the pot. Pour in the white wine or vermouth and top with the tomatoes and olives.

Put the lid on the dish and place it in the oven. Cook for an hour, then remove the lid and cook for a further 10 minutes until the skin of the chicken has crisped up. Check to see if the chicken is done – if you have a thermometer, the internal temperature of the bird should be at least 72°C. The juices should run clear and the legs should feel loose.

Cook the tagliatelle according to the packet instructions. Remove the chicken from the dish and place it on a serving dish, with the tomatoes, olives and onions around it. Squish the flesh out of the garlic cloves and whisk it into the gravy in the casserole dish. Add the tagliatelle to the dish and toss it in the gravy.

Divide the tagliatelle between 4 large pasta bowls and garnish with a few basil leaves. Serve the chicken and tomatoes at the table.

TRAY BAKE CHRISTMAS DINNER

SERVES 4 | PREP: 30 MINS | COOK: ABOUT 1 HOUR

All your Christmas dinner cooked in a couple of roasting tins – how about that? Even Ebenezer Scrooge would have a go at this one. Our festive tray bake includes chicken, pigs in blankets, stuffing balls and veggies and it's fantastic. If you like, you could add Brussels sprouts to the veg – just cut them in half, toss them in oil and add them half way through the cooking time. Serve with some chicken gravy.

4 chicken thighs, bone in
   and skin on
olive oil
1 large onion, sliced into
   wedges
sea salt and black pepper

Stuffing balls
15g butter
1 onion, finely chopped
35g dried cranberries
50ml just-boiled water
50g chestnuts, crumbled
75g breadcrumbs
1 tsp dried thyme
1 egg

Pigs in blankets
4 slices of streaky bacon
8 chipolatas

Vegetables
3 floury potatoes, cut into
   chunks
2 parsnips, cut into chunks
3 carrots, cut into batons
25g lard, dripping or duck fat

To serve
chicken gravy (see p.258)
cranberry relish (see p.132)

Preheat the oven to 200°C/Fan 180°C/Gas 6.

First make the stuffing balls. Melt the butter in a frying pan and add the finely chopped onion. Sauté until very soft and translucent, then remove it from the heat. Put the cranberries in a small bowl, cover with the just-boiled water, then leave to soften and swell. They should absorb all the water but if not, drain them. Put the onions and cranberries in a bowl with the remaining ingredients, then season and mix thoroughly. Shape the mixture into 8 balls.

Next make the pigs in blankets. Cut each piece of bacon in half and stretch each half out with the flat side of a knife. Wrap each stretched half around a chipolata.

Season the chicken thighs with salt and pepper and rub the skins with olive oil. Place the onion wedges in the base of a roasting tin and drizzle with oil. Arrange the chicken thighs, pigs in blankets and stuffing balls on top of the onion.

Now prepare the vegetables. Bring a large saucepan of salted water to the boil. Add the potatoes, followed by the parsnips, then the carrots and simmer for 5 minutes. Drain thoroughly. Shake the pan around a bit to fluff up the edges of the potatoes and parsnips.

Put the lard, dripping or duck fat in another roasting tin and place it in the oven. When the fat is smoking hot, remove the tin from the oven and add all the vegetables. Shake the tin to distribute the veg evenly and season with salt and black pepper.

Put both tins in the oven, with the chicken on top and the vegetables below. Roast for 40–45 minutes, checking regularly and turning the tins round to make sure they cook evenly. When everything is piping hot and well browned, remove the tins from the oven. Serve with plenty of gravy and some cranberry relish.

BRAISED CHICKEN WITH SUMMER GREENS

SERVES 4 | PREP: 15 MINS | COOK: ABOUT 1 HOUR

Si: I love cooked lettuce. Dave: I prefer to think of it as summer cabbage! Whatever side you're on, you'll enjoy this – a fabulously fresh one-pot feast and the lettuce does work really well.

1 tbsp olive oil

4 chicken thighs, bone in, skin on

2 little gems, trimmed and halved

15g butter

400g baby new potatoes

2 leeks, sliced into rounds

2 garlic cloves, finely chopped

100ml white wine

1 large tarragon sprig

150ml chicken stock

1 courgette, sliced into rounds

100g peas

100ml double cream

sea salt and black pepper

To serve

1 tbsp finely chopped tarragon

Heat the olive oil in a large lidded sauté pan. Season the chicken thighs with salt and black pepper, then add them to the pan, skin-side down. Fry until the skin is crisp and well browned. Remove the chicken from the pan and set aside.

Add the little gems, cut-side down, and sear them for a couple of minutes until lightly browned. Remove and set aside.

Now add the butter to the pan and let it melt, then stir in the new potatoes and leeks. When they are coated with the butter, stir in the garlic, then pour in the wine and add the tarragon. Cover and leave to braise for 5 minutes. Pour in the stock and season with salt and pepper.

Remove the lid and put the little gems back in the pan. Add the courgette and peas, then arrange the chicken pieces on top of the veg, skin-side up. Bring the liquid to the boil, then turn down the heat and partially cover the pan. Leave to simmer for about 30 minutes, until the vegetables and chicken are tender.

Pour in the cream around the chicken and leave to simmer, uncovered, for a few more minutes until the sauce has reduced. Serve garnished with tarragon.

CHICKEN, BACON & LEEK SUET ROLL

SERVES 4 | PREP: 30 MINS | COOK: 1½-2 HOURS

People forget just how delicious a proper suet roll can be and roly polys aren't just about jam. Do give this a try – it really is good. It's great just as it is, served hot with some veg, but you might like to make a chicken velouté gravy to go with it for an extra-special treat. It's nice cold as well, so if there's any left, there's lunch for you.

Filling
15g butter, melted
2 slender leeks, finely sliced into rounds
250g boneless chicken breast or thigh meat, finely sliced
50g unsmoked bacon, finely diced (optional)
3 tbsp tarragon mustard

Suet pastry
250g self-raising flour, plus extra for dusting
½ tsp salt
50g butter, chilled and diced
75g suet

To serve (optional)
chicken velouté gravy (see p.258)

Start with the filling. Heat the butter in a frying pan. When it has melted, add the leeks and cook, partially covered, until tender. Turn up the heat, add the chicken and bacon and stir-fry until the chicken is lightly browned and just cooked through. Leave to cool.

Next make the suet pastry. Put the flour in a large bowl and add the salt. Add the butter and rub it into the flour with your fingertips, then add the suet and rub that in to break it up a bit. Add just enough water to bring the dough together – it should be quite dry, not sticky. You will need about 100ml.

Lightly flour your work surface and roll out the dough to a rectangle measuring about 30 x 20cm.

Spread the pastry with the mustard, leaving a border around both of the long edges and one of the short ones. Arrange the chicken, bacon and leeks over the mustard. Then wet the edges with water and roll the pastry up, starting at the short end without the border. Seal all the edges.

Butter a large piece of foil and place the suet roll on top of it. Bring the 2 longest edges of foil together and make a loose pleat – don't wrap it tightly as the roll will expand during the cooking time, but make sure it is completely sealed. Tuck the short ends under.

Put the roll in the top of a steamer and steam for at least 90 minutes, making sure you top the water up as necessary. Remove and let it rest for a few minutes, then unwrap and serve with chicken velouté gravy, if you like.

MEXICAN CHICKEN WITH NACHOS

SERVES 4 | PREP: 20 MINS (PLUS MARINATING TIME) | COOK: ABOUT 1 HOUR

4 skinless, boneless chicken
   thighs, diced
zest and juice of 1 lime
2 tbsp olive or coconut oil
1 large onion, diced
1 red pepper, diced
1 green pepper, diced
3 garlic cloves, finely
   chopped
2 tbsp taco seasoning (see
   p.260 or shop-bought)
400g can of chopped
   tomatoes
250g sweetcorn
2–4 tbsp pickled jalapeños,
   roughly chopped, to taste
50g crème fraiche
50g Cheddar cheese, grated
small bunch of coriander,
   chopped
sea salt and black pepper

Topping
100g plain nachos
100g Cheddar cheese, grated
1 tbsp pickled jalapeños,
   roughly chopped

To serve
crème fraiche or soured
   cream
Cheddar cheese, grated
lime wedges

It's hard to get us past a plate of delicious cheesy nachos! We did a beef chilli with a nacho topping a while back and everyone loved it so here's a chicken version, with lovely fresh flavours of lime and pickled jalapeños. You can buy taco seasoning but we have our own recipe on page 260 if you want to go the extra mile and make your own.

Put the diced chicken thighs in a bowl. Add plenty of seasoning, the lime zest and juice and stir to coat. Set aside for half an hour.

Heat the oil in a flameproof casserole dish. Add the onion and peppers and sauté over a medium-high heat until they start to take on some colour and soften. Add the garlic and chicken and continue to cook until the chicken is done.

Add the taco seasoning and stir until the vegetables and chicken are well coated, then season with salt and pepper. Add the tomatoes, corn and as much of the jalapeños to get the level of heat you like. Bring to the boil, then turn down the heat and simmer gently for about 20 minutes until the sauce has reduced down.

Preheat the oven to 200°C/Fan 180°C/Gas 6. Add the crème fraiche, cheese and half the coriander to the pan and stir gently until the cheese has melted.

For the topping, arrange the nachos over the chicken. Mix the cheese with the jalapeños and the rest of the coriander, then sprinkle this on top of the nachos.

Bake in the oven for about 20 minutes until the cheese is melted and browning. Serve with extra crème fraiche and cheese and some lime wedges.

CURRIED CHICKEN PIE

SERVES 4 | PREP: 25 MINS (PLUS COOLING TIME) | COOK: ABOUT 1 HOUR

1 tbsp vegetable or
    coconut oil
1 large onion, diced
1 red pepper, diced
250g butternut squash
    or pumpkin, diced
500g skinless, boneless
    chicken thighs, diced
1 scotch bonnet, finely
    chopped
3 garlic cloves, finely
    chopped
15g root ginger, finely
    chopped
1 tsp dried thyme
1 tbsp mild Caribbean curry
    powder (see p.260 or
    shop-bought)
1 tbsp plain flour
100ml chicken stock or water
200ml coconut milk
sea salt and black pepper

Pastry
300g plain flour, plus extra
    for dusting
½ tsp turmeric
¼ tsp curry powder
150g lard
2–3 tbsp iced water
milk, for brushing

Salsa
2 mangos, peeled and diced
1 red onion
juice and zest of 1 lime
½ scotch bonnet, finely diced
parsley leaves
a few mint sprigs

Chicken curry pies are a big thing in Scotland and we certainly are partial to them. In our recipe, the tasty filling is rich in Caribbean flavours and encased in a double crust of turmeric-yellow pastry, making this a bit like a Jamaican patty in pie form. The fruity salsa is the perfect accompaniment.

To make the filling, heat the oil in a large flameproof casserole dish and add the onion, pepper and squash. Cook for several minutes until the onion is starting to look translucent, then add the chicken, scotch bonnet, garlic and ginger. Season with salt and pepper. Stir until the chicken is browned, then add the thyme, curry powder and flour. Stir until a paste forms around the chicken and vegetables.

Stir in the stock or water, followed by the coconut milk. Bring to the boil, then turn down the heat and cook, stirring regularly, until the vegetables and chicken are cooked through and the sauce has reduced down – this will take about 15 minutes. Leave to cool completely.

To make the pastry, mix the flour, turmeric and curry powder with half a teaspoon of salt. Rub in the lard, then add just enough iced water to make a smooth dough. Wrap the pastry and chill it until you are ready to roll it out.

Preheat the oven to 200°C/Fan 180°C/Gas 6. Take two-thirds of the pastry and roll it out on a floured work surface. Use it to line a pie dish, then add the cooled filling. Brush the edges of the pastry with water.

Roll out the remaining pastry and place it over the filling. Press all around the edges to seal and crimp them together. Brush the pastry with milk. Bake for about 30 minutes until the pie is golden brown around the edges and piping hot.

For the salsa, mix everything together and season with salt and pepper. Serve the pie with the salsa on the side.

CHICKEN KATSU BURGERS

SERVES 4 | PREP: 20 MINS (PLUS DRAINING TIME FOR VEG) | COOK: 10 MINS

Another bit of fusion here – Japanese katsu meets a burger and lives happily ever after. With the curried mayo and the slaw this is a cracking dish that will keep everyone happy. To make the chicken extra tender, you might want to brine it after slicing and flattening. Dissolve 20 grams of salt in a bowl of about 200ml of water, add the chicken and leave it for about 30 minutes. Then proceed with the recipe.

2 large chicken breasts
50g plain flour
2 eggs
50g panko breadcrumbs
2 tbsp olive oil
15g butter
sea salt and black pepper

Curried burger sauce
4 tbsp mayonnaise
1 tbsp ketchup
1 tbsp lime juice
1 tsp mustard powder
1 tsp hot curry powder
1 tsp soy sauce

Coleslaw
1 carrot, cut into matchsticks
 or grated
75g white cabbage, shredded
4 radishes, sliced into
 matchsticks
½ small onion, finely chopped
1 tsp caster sugar

To serve
4 burger buns, preferably
 brioche
4 large lettuce leaves
4 slices of tomato
1 tbsp sesame seeds

First make the curried burger sauce by mixing all the ingredients together and seasoning with salt and pepper.

Next make the coleslaw. Sprinkle the vegetables with salt and the sugar and place them in a colander over a bowl. Leave to stand for half an hour until some liquid has collected in the bowl and the vegetables have slightly collapsed down. Mix a tablespoon of the curried burger sauce into the vegetables, then set aside.

Cut each chicken breast in half horizontally, to give 4 thin escalopes. To do this, lay each breast on a chopping board, put your hand flat on top and slice through the breast from one side to the other. Put each breast half between 2 sheets of cling film and beat to flatten out. Season with salt and pepper.

Put the flour, eggs and breadcrumbs in 3 separate bowls. Dip a breast half in the flour, pat off any excess, then dip in the beaten eggs. Finally, drop it on to the breadcrumbs and turn it over, making sure it is completely coated. Repeat with the remaining pieces of chicken.

Heat the oil and butter in a frying pan and fry the chicken for 2–3 minutes on each side until the coating is crisp and golden and the chicken is cooked through.

To assemble, lightly toast the burger buns on the cut side only. Spread the bottom half with some of the sauce, then add the lettuce and tomato. Place a piece of chicken on top, followed by the coleslaw. Sprinkle over a few sesame seeds and cover with the top bun. Serve immediately.

MARGARITA CHICKEN FAJITAS

SERVES 4 | PREP: 15 MINS (PLUS MARINATING TIME) | COOK: 30 MINS

400g skinless, boneless
 chicken breast or thigh
 meat, thinly sliced
zest of 1 lime
juice of ½ lime
1 tsp orange zest
2 jalapeños or other green
 chillies, finely chopped
2 tbsp tequila
1 tsp triple sec (optional)
sea salt and black pepper

Fajitas
bunch of coriander
juice of 1 lime
1 tbsp oil
1 onion, sliced into slim
 wedges
1 green pepper, thinly sliced
2 garlic cloves, finely
 chopped
1 tsp cumin seeds
¼ tsp cinnamon
2 tsp chilli paste

To serve
1 red onion, finely sliced
juice of 2 limes
2 avocados
warmed tortillas
green chillies, finely chopped
coriander leaves
lime wedges

This is a union between two of our favourite things and it's not just a gimmick – the margarita ingredients of lime, tequila and triple sec work brilliantly with the chicken and make remarkably tasty fajitas. Allow time to marinate the chicken and the rest is easy. A cocktail in a wrap.

First marinate the chicken. Season the slices with salt and pepper. Put the lime zest and juice, orange zest, chillies, tequila and triple sec, if using, in a bowl and add the slices of chicken. Toss and cover, then leave in the fridge for at least an hour or overnight. Remove from the fridge half an hour before cooking.

Roughly chop the coriander and put it in a food processor or blender with the lime juice. Process until you have a green-flecked sauce. Set aside. Heat the oil in a large sauté pan. Add the onion and green pepper and cook over a medium-high heat until they have started to soften and brown. Add the garlic, cumin seeds, cinnamon and chilli paste and stir for a couple of minutes. Strain the chicken from the marinade and add it to the pan. Sauté over a high heat until cooked through. Add the coriander and lime sauce and toss to coat the chicken. Leave the pan on the heat until the sauce is just heated through.

Put the red onion in a small bowl and cover with half the lime juice and plenty of salt. Leave to stand until the onion has turned bright pink. Put a generous pinch of salt in a separate bowl and add the remaining lime juice. Mash in the avocado to make a rough guacamole.

Serve the chicken with the warmed tortillas and guacamole, garnished with the drained red onion slices, chillies, coriander leaves and lime wedges.

CHICKEN GUMBO

SERVES 4 | PREP: 20 MINS | COOK: ABOUT 1½ HOURS

Gumbo comes from the US state of Louisiana and is a delicious, hearty, soupy stew that's often thickened with okra. We like to make it with chicken on the bone for extra flavour, then strip the meat off the bones once cooked. You can buy the special Cajun seasoning in the supermarket or make your own from our recipe on page 261.

1 tbsp olive or vegetable oil
600g chicken thighs, bone in and skin on
250g smoked sausage, sliced
1 large onion, finely chopped
2 celery sticks, finely chopped
1 green pepper, finely diced
2 garlic cloves, finely chopped
2 tbsp Cajun seasoning (see p.261 or shop-bought)
2 bay leaves
750ml chicken stock
200g okra, trimmed and halved
a few dashes of hot sauce (optional)
200g large, shelled raw prawns (optional)
sea salt and black pepper

Roux
25ml olive oil
25g butter
50g flour

To serve
long-grain rice (see p.262)
hot sauce

First heat the oil in a flameproof casserole dish or a large saucepan. Add the chicken thighs, skin-side down, and fry until the skin is a rich brown. Remove from the pan, then add the sausage slices and sear them briefly. Remove and set aside, then add the onion, celery and green pepper. Sauté over a fairly gentle heat, stirring from time to time, until very soft and translucent.

While the vegetables are softening, make the roux. Put the oil and butter in a small saucepan. When the butter has melted, add the flour and stir to make a paste, then keep stirring until the roux is a rich ochre colour. This will take up to 15 minutes and you must stir throughout to make sure the roux doesn't burn. When the roux has a good colour, remove the pan from the heat and set aside.

Go back to the veg. When they are soft, stir in the roux, then add the garlic, Cajun seasoning and bay leaves. Season with salt and pepper. Pour in the stock and bring to the boil, stirring constantly to make sure all the elements are combined.

Put the chicken back in the pan with the vegetables. Turn down the heat and simmer gently for about 45 minutes, stirring every so often, until the chicken is so tender it's falling off the bones. Add the sausage and okra to the pan and continue to simmer until the okra is cooked to your liking – you can leave it quite al dente, or let it collapse into the gumbo which will help thicken it. Taste for seasoning and add salt, pepper and/or hot sauce as necessary. If including prawns, add them now and simmer until just cooked through.

Remove the chicken from the gumbo, pull the meat off the bones and chop it roughly. Put the meat back in the pan and stir to combine. Serve the gumbo over bowlfuls of rice, with more hot sauce for adding at the table.

CHICKEN FESENJAN

SERVES 4 | PREP: 15 MINS | COOK: ABOUT 1¼ HOURS

We're always on the look out for new spicy dishes and we were really chuffed to discover this fantastic Iranian recipe. It's flavoured with walnuts and pomegranate molasses and it's gently piquant rather than hot, so should appeal to all you korma lovers out there. If you want a bit more heat, add the chilli or cayenne.

2 tbsp olive oil
6-8 skinless chicken pieces
   on the bone (thighs,
   drumsticks or breasts on
   the bone but halved)
2 large onions, thickly sliced
200g walnut halves, finely
   ground
½ tsp cinnamon
½ tsp ground cardamom
½ tsp turmeric
½ tsp chilli powder or
   cayenne (optional)
pinch of saffron, soaked
   in 2 tbsp warm water
   (optional)
500ml chicken stock
100ml pomegranate
   molasses
1 tsp caster sugar or honey
sea salt and black pepper

To serve
parsley or mint leaves,
   to garnish
rice (see p.262)

Heat the oil in a large saucepan or a flameproof casserole dish. Add the chicken pieces and fry them briefly on both sides until brown. Remove the chicken from the pan and add the onions. Cook the onions over a medium-high heat until lightly golden, then stir in the ground walnuts. Continue to cook, stirring constantly, until the walnuts are starting to smell lightly toasted. Stir in the spices and some chilli or cayenne, if using, and season with salt and black pepper.

Pour in the saffron with its water, if using, followed by the stock and bring to the boil, stirring to lift any sticky bits from the base of the pan. Put the chicken back in the pan and turn down the heat. Leave to simmer, uncovered, for up to half an hour until the chicken is tender.

Add the pomegranate molasses to the pan, along with the caster sugar or honey. Continue to simmer for another 20 minutes until the sauce is reduced and is a rich brown in colour. Garnish with parsley or mint and serve with rice.

CHICKEN BRAISED WITH BACON, RED WINE & TOMATOES

SERVES 4 | PREP: 15 MINS | COOK: ABOUT 1 HOUR

This is a version of the hugely popular dish known as chicken cacciatore, or hunter's chicken, but with bacon and mushrooms and it's a perfect robust supper for a cold winter's evening. We'd eat it in summer too! Nice with some roast new potatoes on the side.

1 tbsp olive oil

4 chicken legs or 8 thighs, skin on, bone in

100g bacon lardons

150g chestnut mushrooms, halved

1 large onion, cut into wedges

3 garlic cloves, finely chopped

1 large thyme sprig

2 bay leaves

100ml red wine

400g can of tomatoes

sea salt and black pepper

To serve

handful of parsley, chopped

roast new potatoes with garlic & rosemary (see p.270)

Heat the olive oil in a large lidded sauté pan or a flameproof casserole dish. Season the chicken pieces with salt and pepper, then brown them on both sides. This will take at least 7–8 minutes on the skin side, then a couple minutes more on the reverse.

Remove the chicken from the pan and set aside, then add the bacon, mushrooms and onion. Fry over a medium heat until the bacon is crisp and brown and the mushrooms and onion have softened. Stir in the garlic and add the herbs. Pour in the red wine and bring to the boil, scraping the bottom of the pan with a wooden spoon to lift any sticky caramelised bits.

Add the tomatoes and season with salt and pepper. Put the chicken pieces back in the pan and push them into the sauce. Bring to the boil and simmer, partially covered, for about half an hour until the chicken is tender and close to falling off the bone.

Serve with a sprinkling of parsley and some potatoes.

DUCK LEGS BRAISED WITH LENTILS

SERVES 4 | PREP: 15 MINS | COOK: ABOUT 1 HOUR

Duck and lentils are perfect partners and a traditional combo in France. Duck legs are a lot cheaper than breasts and this is an easy dish to put together but actually tastes a bit special. You can use ready-cooked lentils for speed, but if you want to cook your own, put 160g in a pan of water, bring to the boil and boil fiercely for 10 minutes. Drain and use as below.

2 tbsp olive oil

4 duck legs

1 large onion, diced

1 large carrot, diced

100g celeriac (or 2 celery sticks), diced

3 garlic cloves

a few rosemary sprigs

2 bay leaves

1 large piece of pared orange zest

1 tsp juniper berries, lightly crushed

150ml red wine

2 tsp Dijon mustard

250ml chicken stock

300g cooked Puy lentils

sea salt and black pepper

Heat a tablespoon of the oil in a large frying pan. Season the duck legs with salt, then fry them over a medium-high heat, skin-side down, until much of the fat has rendered out and the skin is a rich brown colour. Turn over and cook on the other side for a few more minutes, then set aside. Reserve the fat.

Put the remaining oil in a large flameproof casserole dish or a lidded sauté pan. Add a tablespoon of the rendered duck fat, then add the onion, carrot and celeriac. Sauté until the onion is starting to look translucent and the vegetables are beginning to brown, then add the garlic. Cook for another couple of minutes, then add the herbs, orange zest and juniper berries. Season with salt and pepper.

Pour in the wine and bring to the boil. Stir in the mustard, then add the stock and lentils and bring back to the boil. Turn down the heat and place the duck legs on the lentils, skin-side up. Cook, partially covered, until the vegetables and duck legs are tender and the sauce has reduced down – this will take about half an hour. Good with some greens.

PORK, LAMB & BEEF

CHINESE ROAST BELLY PORK

SERVES 4 | PREP: 15 MINS (PLUS MARINATING TIME) | COOK: UP TO 3½ HOURS

What's not to love here? Classic Chinese flavours plus sensational crackling - everyone's favourite bit - make this a Sunday roast with an Asian twist. The potatoes are cooked with the pork and soak up the juices beautifully. You won't be able to stop eating them.

1 piece of boned belly pork (about 1.5kg), scored
2 tsp Chinese five-spice powder
600g waxy potatoes, cut into chunks
1 onion, finely chopped
1 garlic bulb, broken into cloves
3 star anise
2 tbsp soy sauce
50ml mirin
sea salt and black pepper

Pat the pork dry and rub salt on to the skin and into the score lines. Mix more salt and pepper with the Chinese five-spice and rub this over the flesh (not on the skin). Leave the meat in the fridge for at least 2 hours, preferably overnight. Take the pork out of the fridge, pat it dry again and bring up to room temperature.

Preheat the oven to 220°C/Fan 200°C/Gas 7. Spread the potatoes over the base of a roasting tin, then sprinkle them with the onion, garlic cloves and star anise. Season with salt. Mix the soy sauce and mirin with 100ml of water and pour the mixture over the potatoes. Place the pork on top.

Roast in the oven for 20 minutes, then reduce the temperature to 180°C/Fan 160°C/Gas 4 and continue to roast for a further 2 hours. The pork should be tender, with much of the fat rendered out, and the skin should be very crisp and slightly blistered. If the pork isn't quite done, leave it for another 20-30 minutes.

Remove the pork from the oven and leave it to rest. Strain off any liquid to serve as a thin gravy. Remove the garlic cloves and either squeeze the flesh out of the skins and whisk it into the liquid, or leave them to serve as they are. Put the roasting tin back in the oven for 20-25 minutes so that the now exposed potatoes can crisp up.

Serve the pork thickly sliced with the gravy, potatoes and perhaps some Chinese greens on the side.

PORK & KIMCHI STEW

SERVES 4 | PREP: 20 MINS (PLUS MARINATING TIME) | COOK: ABOUT 1 HOUR

We both love Korean food, and kimchi and other ingredients, such as gochujang chilli paste and gochugaru chilli flakes, are in supermarkets now. This is a great dish and bear in mind that it will be as spicy as your kimchi – some kimchi are very mild, while others have a lot of heat. If your kimchi is hot, use less chilli paste. If you want to make your own kimchi, have a look at our recipe on page 264.

750g diced pork (shoulder
   or leg)
2 tbsp gochujang chilli paste
1 tbsp vegetable oil
1 large onion, thickly sliced
1 large carrot, cut into
   chunks
2 turnips, cut into wedges
10g dried shiitake
   mushrooms, soaked
   in warm water
200g kimchi
1 tbsp soy sauce
300ml chicken stock
   or water
bunch of spring onions,
   roughly sliced (including
   the green parts)
sea salt and black pepper

To serve
basmati or long-grain rice
   (see p.262)
coriander leaves
1 tsp sesame seeds
chilli flakes (preferably
   gochugaru)

Put the pork in a bowl and season it with salt and pepper. Add the gochujang paste and stir until the pork is completely coated. Leave to marinate for half an hour.

Heat the oil in a large flameproof casserole dish. Add the onion, carrot and turnips and fry over a high heat until they start to brown, stirring regularly. Add the pork and continue to fry until browned.

Drain the mushrooms, reserving their soaking liquor, chop them roughly and add them to the casserole dish. Strain the liquor and add this too, along with the kimchi and soy sauce. Add the stock or water, bring it to the boil, then turn down the heat. Cover and leave to simmer until the pork is tender. Remove the lid and leave to simmer until the sauce has reduced.

Add the spring onions and leave to simmer until they start to soften. Serve with rice and garnish with coriander leaves, sesame seeds and a few extra chilli flakes, depending on the heat of your kimchi.

PIGS IN BLANKETS TOAD IN THE HOLE

SERVES 4 | PREP: 20 MINS (PLUS TIME FOR BATTER TO STAND) | COOK: ABOUT 1 HOUR

We love Yorkshires with anything and this is a great way of getting them into your Christmas dinner. We thought it was impossible to reinvent the much-loved toad in the hole. But then it came to us – some say the best part of Christmas is the pigs in blankets, so you've guessed it! We've come up with this genius idea, which could be just the job for a Boxing Day brunch. Serve with cranberry relish and some gravy, if you like.

Cranberry relish
250g cranberries (fresh or frozen)
100g caster sugar
juice of 1 orange
1 tsp orange zest
50ml port (optional)
pinch of salt

Yorkshire pudding batter
150g plain flour
1 tsp dried thyme
2 eggs
275ml whole milk
sea salt and black pepper

Pigs in blankets
dripping or oil
8 slices of streaky bacon
1 tbsp mustard (optional)
24 cocktail sausages or 12 chipolatas, halved

To serve (optional)
onion gravy (see p.258)

First make the cranberry relish. Put all the ingredients in a saucepan and stir over a low heat until all the sugar has dissolved. Turn up the heat until the mixture is just boiling and continue to cook until at least half the cranberries have burst. Remove the pan from the heat and leave the relish to cool – the consistency will thicken and become jammy.

To make the Yorkshire batter, put the flour in a bowl with plenty of seasoning and the thyme. Whisk in the eggs to make a thick, yellow paste, then gradually work in the milk until you have a smooth, thyme-flecked batter. Alternatively, put everything in a food processor or blender and whizz until smooth. Leave the batter to stand for an hour.

Preheat the oven to 200°C/Fan 180°C/Gas 6. Put a knob of dripping or a splash of oil into each hole of a 12-hole muffin tin and heat. Stretch out the streaky bacon rashers and cut each one into 3 pieces. Spread the bacon with mustard, if using, and wrap a piece around each cocktail sausage. Remove the tin from the oven and add 2 pigs in blankets to each hole. Put the tin back in the oven and cook for 20–25 minutes until they look nicely browned.

Remove the tin from the oven and divide the batter between the 12 holes. Return to the oven and cook for a further 20 minutes. When done, the puddings should be puffed up around the edges and a rich brown. Serve with the cranberry relish and onion gravy, if you like.

If you prefer to make one large toad in the hole, cook the pigs in blankets in a large roasting tin. Add the batter and then cook for another 30–35 minutes.

SAUSAGE & SAUERKRAUT CASSEROLE

SERVES 4 | PREP: 15 MINS | COOK: 35-40 MINS

Sausage and sauerkraut are perfect partners. They belong together – well, like we do! This can be made with smoked sausage if you prefer but it's great with regular British bangers. Good with mash and copious amounts of beer.

2 tbsp olive oil

8 pork sausages

1 large onion, sliced

2 garlic cloves, finely chopped

1 tbsp wholegrain mustard

½ small green cabbage, (about 200g), shredded (optional)

300g sauerkraut, drained and squeezed out

1 eating apple, peeled and diced

200ml chicken stock

sea salt and black pepper

Heat the oil in a large, lidded sauté pan. Add the sausages and brown them all over, then remove them from the pan and set aside. Add the onion and cook for several minutes until it starts to soften, then add the garlic, mustard and green cabbage, if using. Continue to cook, stirring regularly, until the cabbage has collapsed down but is still a bright green.

Stir in the sauerkraut and apple, then pour in the stock. Season with salt and pepper. Put the sausages back in the pan, placing them on top of the cabbage and sauerkraut.

Continue to cook very gently, uncovered, until the sausages are cooked through and the liquid has reduced – the mixture should be relatively dry. This should take 15–20 minutes. Nice served with some mashed potatoes.

MERGUEZ SAUSAGES WITH THREE-ROOT MASH

SERVES 4 | PREP: 20 MINS | COOK: ABOUT 50 MINS

This is bangers and mash for the 21st century! The combination of the spicy sausages, rich tomato gravy and the three-root mash with a touch of preserved lemon works brilliantly and if you want some extra heat, add the harissa. It's well worth steaming the veg for the mash, rather than boiling, as it really does give a better result.

1 tbsp olive oil
8–12 merguez sausages
  (depending on size)
1 large red onion, finely sliced
1 tbsp harissa paste
  (optional)
½ tsp cinnamon
zest of ½ lemon
400g can of chopped
  tomatoes
200ml vegetable or chicken
  stock or water
a few mint sprigs, to garnish
sea salt and black pepper

Three-root mash
200g carrots, cut into
  2cm dice
250g celeriac, cut into
  3cm dice
250g floury potatoes,
  cut into 4cm dice
25g butter
1 tbsp finely chopped
  preserved lemon
small bunch of parsley,
  finely chopped

Start with the sausages. Heat the oil in a large sauté pan. Add the sausages and brown them on all sides. Remove them from the pan and set them aside, then pour off most of the fat which will have rendered out of the sausages. Leave a couple of tablespoons in the pan.

Add the slices of onion and sauté them over a medium-high heat until they start to brown. Add the harissa paste, if using, and cook for a couple of minutes. Add the cinnamon and lemon zest, then pour in the tomatoes. Rinse out the tomato can with the stock and add the stock to the pan.

Season with salt and pepper and bring to the boil. Turn down the heat and simmer for about 15 minutes until the sauce has reduced by about a third. Put the sausages back in the pan and simmer until they are cooked through.

While the sauce is simmering, make the mash. Put freshly boiled water into a saucepan and set it over a high heat. Arrange the vegetables in a steamer basket: the carrots at the bottom, followed by the celeriac, then the potato. Season with salt. Place the steamer over the saucepan and cover, then steam for about 20 minutes until the vegetables are tender.

Remove the vegetables from the steamer and mash them well. Heat the butter in a pan and stir it into the mash, along with the preserved lemon and the parsley.

Serve the sausages in the tomato gravy, garnished with a few mint sprigs, with the mash on the side.

CUMBERLAND SAUSAGE PIE

SERVES 4 | PREP: 20 MINS | COOK: ABOUT 1½ HOURS

Cumberland pie is very similar to shepherd's pie, so we thought to ourselves: why not make a pie with Cumberland sausages for the full Cumberland experience? We've broken the sausages up into little balls so everyone gets a bite of banger satisfaction. Add the cheesy potato topping and this is a dish to be proud of.

8 Cumberland sausages
 (about 500g)
3 tbsp olive oil
15g butter
1 large onion, diced
2 large carrots, diced
2 celery sticks, diced
1 tbsp plain flour
2 tbsp tomato purée
100ml red wine
400ml beef stock
1 tsp Worcestershire sauce
2 bay leaves
1 large thyme sprig
1–2 tbsp Cumberland sauce
1 tsp orange zest (optional)
sea salt and black pepper

Topping
1kg floury potatoes, cut
 into chunks
30g butter
1 bunch of spring onions,
 cut into rounds
1 tbsp Dijon mustard
 (optional)
50ml single cream
100g Cheddar cheese, grated

Skin the sausages. Divide each sausage into 4 and roll each piece into balls. Heat a tablespoon of olive oil and lightly fry the sausage balls until browned on all sides, then set them aside.

Heat the remaining oil and the butter in a large saucepan or a flameproof casserole dish. Add the vegetables and sauté them for a few minutes, until well coated with the oil and butter. Cover and leave to cook, stirring regularly, until tender – this will take at least 10 minutes.

Stir in the flour, then when it has disappeared into the oil, stir in the tomato purée. Turn up the heat and cook for a couple of minutes, stirring constantly, then pour in the red wine. Bring to the boil and continue to stir, then add the stock, Worcestershire sauce and herbs. Stir in the Cumberland sauce and the orange zest, if using, then add the sausage balls. Season with plenty of salt and pepper.

Bring to the boil, then turn down to a simmer. Cook the sauce for 20 minutes, stirring every so often to make sure it doesn't catch on the bottom, until it has reduced down a bit and thickened.

Meanwhile, make the topping. Bring a large saucepan of water to the boil. Add the potatoes, season with plenty of salt and cook for 10-15 minutes until the potatoes are tender. Preheat the oven to 200°C/Fan 180°C/Gas 6.

Drain the potatoes and mash until smooth. Melt the butter in a saucepan and add the spring onions. Fry until they start to soften, then add the potatoes to the pan with the mustard, if using, and the cream. Beat together until well combined.

Put the filling into a pie dish or casserole dish. Spread the mashed potato over the top, then rough it up with a fork. Sprinkle with cheese. Bake in the oven for about 30 minutes until well browned and piping hot.

LAMB & AUBERGINE CASSEROLE

SERVES 4 | PREP: 20 MINS | COOK: UP TO 2 HOURS

Lamb and aubergine combine beautifully in this simple casserole with a Middle Eastern vibe. Neck fillet is probably the most tender cut to use, but shoulder or leg will also work really well. Good served with rice or couscous or try the white bean salad on page 268.

3 tbsp olive oil

2 large aubergines, cut
 into large chunks

1 large onion, diced

500g lamb neck fillet, leg
 or shoulder, diced and
 trimmed

3 garlic cloves, finely
 chopped

1 large thyme sprig

1 large oregano sprig or
 2 tsp dried oregano

½ tsp cinnamon

200ml red wine

400g can of chopped
 tomatoes

2 pieces of pared lemon zest

2 roasted red peppers, cut
 into strips

small bunch of parsley, finely
 chopped, to garnish

small bunch of mint, finely
 chopped, to garnish

sea salt and black pepper

To serve (optional)
white bean salad (see p.268)

Heat 2 tablespoons of the oil in a large flameproof casserole dish. Sauté the aubergine chunks over a high heat until browned on all sides. Remove them from the pan and add the remaining oil. Add the onion and lamb and sauté until the lamb is seared on all sides and the onion has started to brown and turn translucent.

Add the garlic, herbs and cinnamon and cook for another couple of minutes, then add the wine. Bring to the boil, then add the tomatoes and lemon zest. Season with salt and pepper. Bring to the boil, then turn down the heat and cover. Leave to simmer for an hour.

Put the aubergine back in the casserole dish and add the peppers. Continue to cook, this time uncovered, until the aubergines have softened and the meat is completely tender – this will take another half an hour. Garnish with the herbs and serve with the white bean salad.

SLOW-ROAST SHOULDER OF LAMB

SERVES 4 | PREP: 15 MINS | COOK: UP TO 4 HOURS & 20 MINS

Don't be alarmed by the cooking time. There's actually very little work to do here and once the lamb is in the oven you can just leave it to look after itself while you relax. After all those hours in the oven the lamb will be very relaxed too – meltingly soft, tender meat. Fabulous.

1 x 1.5–2kg lamb shoulder,
    on the bone
1 tbsp olive oil
1 tsp dried oregano
½ tsp cinnamon
2 red onions, sliced
    into wedges
1 lemon, sliced
1 garlic bulb, separated
    into unpeeled cloves
3 or 4 rosemary sprigs
2 oregano sprigs
3 bay leaves
250ml white wine
2 tbsp capers
2 tbsp chopped green olives
up to 1 tsp honey (optional)
sea salt and black pepper

To serve (optional)
roast new potatoes with
    garlic and rosemary
    (see p.270)

Preheat the oven to 220°C/Fan 200°C/Gas 7.

Rub the skin of the lamb shoulder with olive oil. Sprinkle over the oregano and cinnamon and season with plenty of salt and pepper.

Spread the onions, lemon, garlic and herbs over the base of a large roasting tin, placing the garlic in the centre to make sure it is covered by the lamb. Put the lamb shoulder on top. Pour the white wine and 100ml of water around the meat.

Roast for 20 minutes to give the lamb a chance to develop a crust, then turn the heat down to 150°C/Fan 130°C/Gas 2. Roast for 2½–4 hours, depending on the size of your joint. Start checking after 2½ hours – when the lamb is ready the bone will feel loose and the meat will be very soft and tender.

Remove the tin from the oven and place the lamb on a warmed serving platter. Cover with foil. Strain the contents of the roasting dish and add the onions and lemon slices to the platter. Push everything else – including the garlic – through a sieve, then cool until the fat settles on top – this won't take long. Transfer the strained juices to a saucepan and place over a medium heat to warm through. Taste for seasoning and add salt and pepper. Stir in the capers and olives and add the honey if the sauce is too astringent.

Serve the lamb with the sauce at the table and some roast new potatoes.

QUICK BEEF RENDANG

SERVES 4 | PREP: 20 MINS | COOK: 25-30 MINS

This has the great flavour of a rendang, but the speed of a balti, so the best of both worlds. Bavette or flank steak is very tasty and is cheaper than the posher cuts of steak but still tender if you cook it right. Do try our rendang paste but you can buy some if you prefer.

Rendang paste

3 lemongrass stalks

6 garlic cloves

25g root ginger, peeled
  and roughly chopped

25g galangal, peeled and
  roughly chopped (optional)

4 Thai chillies, roughly
  chopped (deseeded if
  you prefer)

Curry

800g bavette or flank steak,
  thickly sliced across the
  grain

1-2 tbsp coconut or
  vegetable oil

bouquet garni made up of
  1 cinnamon stick, 4 cloves,
  3 star anise, 8 lime leaves

2 onions, finely sliced

200g can of coconut milk

1 tbsp soft light brown sugar

2 tsp tamarind paste

2 tbsp soy sauce or
  Thai fish sauce

juice of 1-2 limes

sea salt and black pepper

To serve

4 lime leaves, finely sliced

fresh coriander leaves

green chillies, sliced

rotis

First make the paste. Put everything in a food processor with 50ml of water and blitz until quite smooth and liquid.

Season the beef with salt and pepper. Heat the oil in a wok or a large, shallow pan and sear the meat quickly on all sides until it is well browned. It's best to do this in a few batches – don't be tempted to try to brown it all at once, as the pan will be too crowded and the meat will start to steam. Remove the meat from the pan.

Add more oil if necessary, then add the bouquet garni and the onions and fry briskly until the onions are a light golden brown. Pour in the paste and stir until very aromatic. Put the beef back in the pan and stir to coat with the paste.

Add the coconut milk, sugar, tamarind paste and soy sauce or fish sauce. Season with salt and black pepper, then bring to the boil. Turn down the heat to a fast simmer, then leave to cook for about 10-15 minutes until the coconut milk has reduced by about half. Add half the lime juice and stir, then taste. Adjust the flavour by adding more salt, lime juice or sugar to get the taste you like.

Stir in the sliced lime leaves, then serve sprinkled with coriander leaves and chillies, with some rotis on the side.

MONGOLIAN BEEF STIR-FRY

SERVES 2 | PREP: 15 MINS (PLUS MARINATING TIME) | COOK: 15 MINS

The idea is to get all the veggies and bits and bobs chopped and ready while the meat is marinating, then get your wok out and go for it. The brief marinade makes this economical cut of meat beautifully tender, then it's cooked quickly and your dinner for two is ready.

Beef and marinade

300g beef (preferably
  bavette or flank steak)

1 tbsp soy sauce

1 tsp sesame oil

2 tbsp cornflour

sea salt and black pepper

Sauce

2 tbsp soy sauce

2 tbsp mirin

2 tbsp rice vinegar

1 tbsp hoisin sauce

2 tsp sriracha or similar
  chilli sauce

Stir-fry

3 tbsp vegetable oil

1 large head of broccoli, cut
  into florets and blanched
  for 2 minutes

1 bunch of spring onions,
  cut into 3cm lengths

15g root ginger, cut into
  matchsticks

2 garlic cloves, chopped

1 tsp sesame seeds,
  to garnish

To serve

basmati or long-grain rice
  (see p.262)

Slice the beef into very thin strips across the grain. Put these in a bowl with the soy sauce and sesame oil. Season and toss, allowing the soy to soak into the beef, then sprinkle over the cornflour. Toss until the strips are completely coated, then lay them out on a chopping board or on kitchen paper – this will stop them from going sticky as they marinate. Leave for 20 minutes.

Mix all the sauce ingredients together and set aside.

When you are ready to cook the stir-fry, heat a tablespoon of oil in a wok. When it is shimmering, add half the beef and stir-fry very quickly until seared on all sides. Remove with a slotted spoon. Add a little more oil if necessary, then repeat with the rest of the beef.

Add the remaining oil to the wok. Add the broccoli and stir-fry for 2 minutes, then add the spring onions, ginger and garlic. Continue to stir fry for a further 2 minutes then return the beef to the wok. Pour over the sauce and continue to stir until everything is coated in the sauce. Leave it to bubble for a couple of minutes, then divide the meat and vegetables between 2 bowls and sprinkle with sesame seeds. Serve immediately with rice.

TEX-MEX BEEF CHILLI

SERVES 4 | PREP: 15 MINS | COOK: ABOUT 2½ HOURS

The idea for this one came from a chilli dish we cooked on our Route 66 television show a few years ago. It's really rich and substantial with lots of flavour from the stout and coffee. A proper chilli that's good enough for any cowhand.

2 tbsp olive oil or lard

750g stewing or braising
   steak, diced

2 onions, finely chopped

4 garlic cloves, finely
   chopped

3 jalapeño chillies, finely
   chopped (depending on
   how hot you want it)

2–3 tsp chilli powder
   (depending on how hot
   you want it)

1 tsp smoked chilli powder,
   such as chipotle

1 tbsp ground cumin

1 tbsp ground coriander

1 tsp ground cinnamon

1 tbsp dried oregano

2 tbsp light brown sugar

2 tbsp tomato purée

400g can of tomatoes

100ml strong coffee

250ml stout

2 x 400g cans of red kidney
   beans, drained

sea salt and black pepper

To serve (optional)

chillies, sliced

Cheddar cheese, grated

soured cream

tortilla chips

Heat half the oil or lard in a large flameproof casserole dish. Season the meat with salt and pepper, and sear it until well browned – it's best to do this in a few batches so you don't overcrowd the pan. Transfer each batch to a plate.

Heat the remaining oil or lard in the casserole dish, then add the onions. Sauté for a few minutes over a medium-high heat, so they take on some colour, then add the garlic, chillies, spices, oregano and sugar. Stir until the spices make a rough paste around the oil, then add the tomato purée. Keep stirring until the purée and oil start to separate. The mixture should smell spicy and slightly caramelised from the sugar.

Put the meat back in the casserole dish and add the tomatoes, coffee and stout. Bring to the boil, stirring everything up from the base of the casserole as you do so, then reduce the heat, partially cover and leave to simmer for an hour.

Add the beans, then check the seasoning. Continue to simmer for at least another hour until the meat is very tender and the sauce well reduced. Serve with chillies, grated cheese, soured cream and tortilla chips, if you like.

STEAK & ASPARAGUS SALAD

SERVES 4 | PREP: 10 MINS | COOK: UP TO 20 MINUTES

A simple but substantial salad, this is a real treat when asparagus is in season. Everything you need is here but you might like some crusty bread on the side and maybe a little tomato and red onion salad as well.

400g salad or baby new
   potatoes
a few mint sprigs
2 sirloin steaks (about
   2cm thick)
bunch of asparagus,
   trimmed
150g salad leaves
small bunch of chives,
   to garnish
sea salt

Dressing
1 tbsp olive oil
2 tbsp crème fraiche
1 tsp mustard
1 tsp sherry vinegar
1 tsp honey
2 tsp black peppercorns,
   crushed

First make the salad dressing. Whisk everything together, season with salt and set aside.

Bring a pan of water to the boil and add salt, the potatoes and mint sprigs. Boil until the potatoes are just tender, then drain thoroughly and set aside.

Meanwhile, heat a large griddle pan. Season the steaks with plenty of salt, then grill them to your liking. For rare, cook for 1½ minutes on the first side, then 1 minute on the second; for medium-rare, cook for 2 minutes on the first side, then 1½ on the second. For medium, cook for 2 minutes on each side.

Remove the steaks and set them aside to rest for 5-10 minutes, then add the asparagus to the griddle and cook, turning regularly until they have char lines and are knife tender.

Slice the rested steak into strips and add any juices to the salad dressing. Arrange the salad leaves, potatoes, steak and asparagus on a large platter and drizzle over the dressing. Snip the chives over the top and serve.

BEEF & BEETROOTS WITH HORSERADISH DUMPLINGS

SERVES 4 | PREP: 20 MINS | COOK: ABOUT 2 HOURS

If you like stew and dumplings try this – it's like a beefy borscht with a dumpling float! Both beef and beetroots work perfectly with horseradish to make this something a bit special for your supper. A real winter warmer.

800g braising or stewing
   steak
2 tbsp plain flour
2 tsp mustard powder
2-3 tbsp beef dripping
   or olive oil
300ml red wine
2 red onions, cut into wedges
2 carrots, cut into chunks
3 medium beetroots, peeled
   and cut into wedges
2 celery sticks, cut into
   chunks
1 large thyme sprig
3 garlic cloves, sliced
1 tsp juniper berries,
   lightly crushed
300ml beef stock
sea salt and black pepper

Dumplings
250g self-raising flour
1 tsp baking powder
125g beef suet
2 tbsp finely chopped dill
2 tbsp horseradish sauce

Pat the steak dry. Put the flour into a bowl with the mustard powder, a teaspoon of salt and plenty of pepper. Toss the beef in the flour, then pat off any excess.

Heat half the dripping or oil in a large flameproof casserole dish. Brown the beef in batches, adding a little more dripping or oil if necessary. Remove the last of the beef and deglaze the casserole with a glug of the red wine, stirring to scrape up any brown bits on the bottom. Pour this off and reserve, then wipe the casserole dish clean.

Heat another tablespoon of oil or dripping and add the vegetables. Fry over a high heat until they start to take on some colour. Add the thyme, garlic and juniper berries, then put the beef back in the casserole dish. Pour over the reserved liquid from deglazing the casserole, then add the rest of the wine and the beef stock. Bring to the boil, then turn down the heat, cover the dish with a lid and leave to simmer gently for 1½ hours. By this time the meat and vegetables should be nice and tender.

To make the dumplings, put the flour, baking powder and suet in a bowl and add plenty of salt. Stir in the dill. Mix the horseradish with 50ml of water, then work this in, followed by just enough water to make a sticky dough – you'll probably need about another 50-75ml. Drop handfuls of this dough on top of the meat and vegetables and simmer for another 20-25 minutes until the dumplings are well risen, shiny and firm. Good with some green veg on the side.

MINCE

BOBOTIE

SERVES 4 | PREP: 15 MINS | COOK: ABOUT 45 MINS

Here's our version of a popular South African dish that has a spicy meat filling topped with a savoury custard. An exotic twist on shepherd's pie and a new favourite of ours.

1 tbsp olive oil
1 large onion, finely chopped
500g beef mince
3 garlic cloves, finely
    chopped
1 tbsp hot curry powder
¼ tsp each of ground
    cinnamon, allspice
    and cloves
2 tbsp chutney, such as
    mango or Pickapeppa
    sauce
1 tsp Worcestershire sauce
35g almonds, chopped
50g sultanas
25g breadcrumbs
up to 350ml milk
3 eggs
¼ tsp turmeric
a few bay leaves, to garnish
sea salt and black pepper

Preheat the oven to 180°C/Fan 160°C/Gas 4.

Heat the oil in a large frying pan or sauté pan. Add the onion and cook until it's soft and translucent. Turn up the heat, add the mince and cook, stirring regularly, until well browned, breaking it up with the back of a wooden spoon.

Turn down the heat and add the garlic, curry powder, spices, chutney, Worcestershire sauce, almonds and sultanas. Season with salt and pepper and cook, stirring constantly, for a couple of minutes. Remove from the heat.

Soak the breadcrumbs in half the milk – they will absorb it very quickly. Strain through a sieve, removing as much of the milk as possible. Add the breadcrumbs and one of the eggs to the beef mixture and mix thoroughly.

Measure the remaining milk and make it up to 250ml. Beat in the turmeric and the remaining 2 eggs and season with salt.

Press the beef mixture into an ovenproof dish, making it as level as possible. Pour the custard mixture over the top and arrange the bay leaves as decoration. Bake in the oven for 25–30 minutes until the custard is just set and well browned – it should still have a slight wobble to it.

LAMB KOFTE VINDALOO

SERVES 4 | PREP: 20 MINS | COOK: ABOUT 40 MINS

We love meatballs and we love a vindaloo curry, so guess what? The lamb kofte vindaloo was born – a glorious fusion of different cuisines! Go on – you know you want to taste this. Nice served with rice or flatbread. If possible, make your own vindaloo paste from our recipe on page 259, or you can buy some – we won't judge. Jaggery, by the way, is a type of sugar that's popular in India and is made of palm tree sap.

Meatballs

1 tbsp olive oil

1 onion, finely chopped

2 garlic cloves, finely
   chopped

500g minced lamb

1 tsp dried oregano

zest of 1 lemon

½ tsp chilli flakes (optional)

25g pine nuts, roughly
   chopped

small bunch of basil,
   finely chopped

75g breadcrumbs

1 egg

sea salt and black pepper

Curry

3 tbsp vegetable or
   coconut oil

3 onions, finely sliced

2–3 tbsp vindaloo spice paste
   (see p.259 or shop-bought)

up to 1 tsp light soft brown
   sugar or jaggery

To serve

green chillies, sliced

coriander leaves

Heat the oven to 200°C/Fan 180°C/Gas 6. Line a baking tray with baking parchment. Put all the meatball ingredients in a bowl and season generously with salt and pepper. Mix the lamb mince very thoroughly until it feels quite stiff, then shape it into 20 balls or torpedo shapes. Place the balls on the baking tray and bake them in the oven for 10 minutes. Remove and set aside.

For the curry, heat the oil in a large saucepan or a flameproof casserole dish. Fry the onions over a medium heat until they're a deep golden brown, then add the vindaloo paste and stir for a few more minutes. Add 600ml of water, plenty of seasoning and half the sugar. Bring to the boil then turn down the heat and simmer for about 20 minutes until the sauce is reduced, but not too thick – it will continue reducing when you add the meatballs. Taste for seasoning and add the rest of the sugar and more salt if necessary.

Add the meatballs to the sauce and continue to simmer gently for another 5–10 minutes until the meatballs are piping hot and the sauce has reduced to a thick gravy. Serve with sliced green chillies and coriander.

SHEPHERD'S PIE WITH COUSCOUS TOPPING

SERVES 4 | PREP: 15 MINS | COOK: ABOUT 1½ HOURS

We know that shepherd's pie is one of the nation's favourite dishes, so we've worked hard to come up with a clever new twist. There's a Middle Eastern flavour to this recipe, with the spicing for the lamb and the couscous topping, which is quick, easy and less carby than mash. The flaked almonds add a nice touch of crunch. Fragrant and delicious.

1 tbsp olive oil
1 onion, finely chopped
2 celery sticks, diced
1 red or green pepper, diced
400g lamb mince
3 garlic cloves, finely
    chopped
1 tbsp ras-el-hanout
½ tsp cayenne, for extra heat
    (optional)
1 tsp dried mint
1 tsp rosemary leaves, finely
    chopped
1 tbsp tomato purée
400g can of chickpeas,
    drained
400g can of tomatoes
200ml chicken or vegetable
    stock
25g dried apricots, chopped
sea salt and black pepper

Topping
125g couscous
150ml warm water
2 tbsp olive oil
35g flaked almonds
handful of chopped parsley
butter, for dotting on top

First make the filling. Heat the olive oil in a large saucepan or a flameproof casserole dish. Add the onion, celery and pepper and cook over a medium heat, stirring regularly, until the onion is soft and translucent. Turn up the heat and add the lamb. Cook until the lamb is well browned, then stir in the garlic, ras-el-hanout, cayenne, if using, the herbs and tomato purée. Stir for 2–3 minutes and season with salt and pepper.

Add the chickpeas, tomatoes, stock and chopped apricots. Bring to the boil, then turn the heat down to a simmer. Cover and cook for half an hour, then remove the lid and continue to simmer for another 10 minutes until the sauce has reduced.

To make the topping, put the couscous in a bowl and season with salt and pepper. Pour over the warm water and add the olive oil. Leave to stand until all the liquid has been absorbed by the couscous. Fluff up with a fork and stir in the flaked almonds and herbs.

Preheat the oven to 200°C/Fan 180°C/Gas 6. Put the filling in a large ovenproof dish – or leave it in the casserole dish if that's what you used. Sprinkle over the couscous in an even layer, then dot with butter. Bake in the preheated oven for 25 minutes until the topping starts to brown.

LINDSTRÖM BURGERS

SERVES 4 | PREP: 15 MINS (PLUS CHILLING TIME) | COOK: 10 MINS

We were very excited to find out about this burger. It's a Swedish classic and named after Henrik Lindström, who came up with this combination of beef, beets and capers, and very good it is too. Traditionally, these are served with an egg on the top and sometimes with sautéed potatoes instead of a bun. A refreshing change from your usual quarter pounder.

Burgers

400g beef mince

1 small red onion, very finely
  chopped

50g pickled beetroot, grated
  or finely chopped

25g capers, rinsed and
  roughly chopped

25g cornichons, finely
  chopped

50g breadcrumbs

1 egg

2 tbsp double cream or
  crème fraiche

sea salt and black pepper

To serve

4 burger buns (rye
  or wholemeal)

4 eggs

4 large lettuce leaves

a few dill sprigs

Dijon mustard (optional)

Put the beef mince in a bowl with all the other burger ingredients and season with plenty of salt and pepper. Mix thoroughly and form into 4 patties. Chill thoroughly, as this will also help the flavours meld together.

Remove the burgers from the fridge half an hour before you are ready to cook.

Heat a frying pan or a griddle to a medium-high heat. Add the burgers and cook them on one side until they come cleanly away from the pan and are nicely charred. Flip and cook on the other side for a further 2–3 minutes until done to your liking.

Lightly toast the burger buns and fry the eggs. Place a large lettuce leaf on the bottom half of each bun, then top with a burger, fried egg, a few snipped dill fronds and a dollop of mustard, if using. Top with the other half of each bun and serve immediately.

CORNED BEEF PASTIES

MAKES 8 | PREP: 20 MINS (PLUS CHILLING TIME) | COOK: ABOUT 1 HOUR

A corned beef pie is a great tradition in the Northeast, so we decided to give it a new life as a pasty. These have all the satisfaction of a traditional pasty but with a luscious filling of corned beef and a dash of ketchup. A great one-stop feast for supper or to take on a picnic. We guarantee these will put a smile on your face.

Pastry
450g plain flour, plus extra
   for dusting
2 tsp baking powder
1 tsp salt
125g butter or 65g butter
   and 60g lard, chilled
   and diced
1 egg yolk
iced water
1 egg, beaten with 1 tbsp
   of water

Filling
100g swede, diced
l00g carrot, diced
200g potato, diced
1 large onion, very finely
   chopped
300g corned beef, diced
2 tbsp tomato ketchup
1 tbsp Dijon mustard
sea salt and black pepper

First make the pastry. Put the flour in a bowl with the baking powder and salt. Add the cubes of butter or butter and lard and rub them in until the mixture resembles very fine breadcrumbs. Add the egg yolk and drizzle in iced water until you have a smooth dough. You will need about 100ml of water, perhaps a little more. Knead the dough lightly until it is smooth, then wrap it in cling film and chill it in the fridge for at least half an hour. You can make the pastry in a food processor or a stand mixer instead of by hand, if you prefer.

To make the filling, bring a small pan of water to the boil and add the swede and carrot. Boil for 5 minutes, then add the potato and boil for a further 5 minutes. The vegetables should be al dente – you don't want them to cook through completely. Drain and cool under cold water.

Put the onion and corned beef into a bowl and season with salt and pepper. Stir in the ketchup and mustard, followed by the cooled vegetables. Preheat the oven to 180°C/Fan 160°C/Gas 4.

Divide the pastry into 8 pieces – this is best done by weighing the portions. Dust your work surface with flour and roll out each piece of dough to a round of about 19cm in diameter. It will be thin and elastic and not as crumbly or fragile as normal shortcrust. Take an eighth of the filling and place it on one half of a round. Brush the edges of the pastry with beaten egg and stretch the uncovered half of pastry over the filled half. Seal the pastry and crimp in whatever style you like. Brush with the beaten egg and cut a couple of slits in the pastry to release steam. Continue until you have made all 8 pasties.

Place the pasties on a couple of baking trays, then bake for 45–50 minutes until the pastry has puffed up a bit and is a rich brown. Remove from the oven and enjoy hot or cold.

CORNED BEEF LANCASHIRE HOTPOT

SERVES 4 | PREP: 20 MINS | COOK: 1¾ HOURS

We've created hotpots in all their glory – a veggie version, a sausage hotpot and now let's welcome the corned beef Lancashire hotpot to the family. Crispy potatoes on the top, soft juicy slices at the bottom and beautiful corned beef in the middle – heaven from a can!

1 tbsp butter, plus extra for greasing and dotting on top

1 tbsp olive oil

2 onions, thinly sliced

1 tbsp flour

500ml beef stock

1 tbsp tomato purée or ketchup

1kg floury potatoes, peeled or unpeeled and thinly sliced

340g can of corned beef, thickly sliced

1 tsp dried thyme

1 tsp dried sage

sea salt and black pepper

Preheat the oven to 180°C/Fan 160°C/Gas 4. Generously butter a large, deep casserole dish.

For the gravy, heat the butter and oil in a large frying pan. Add the onions and fry until they are just starting to soften without taking on any colour. Stir in the flour until a paste forms around the onions, then add the stock and tomato purée or ketchup. Simmer for a few minutes, stirring regularly, until the gravy has thickened slightly.

Arrange a third of the potato slices over the base of the buttered casserole dish and season. Layer on half the corned beef, then sprinkle some of the herbs on top. Season with a little more salt and pepper and pour in half the gravy. Add another third of potatoes, remembering to season as you go, followed by the rest of the corned beef, herbs and gravy. Top with the remaining potatoes and press down lightly. Dot with butter.

Put the lid on the casserole dish and bake in the preheated oven for an hour. Remove the lid and cook for another 30 minutes until the top layer of potatoes has crisped up around the edges and is golden brown. Some green vegetables on the side would be nice.

MEATBALLS WITH DRIED CHERRIES & PISTACHIOS

SERVES 4 | PREP: 25 MINS (PLUS SOAKING TIME) | COOK: 15 MINS

50g dried cherries
500g lamb mince
1 onion, finely chopped
2 garlic cloves, crushed
zest of 1 lime
1 tsp dried mint
½ tsp cinnamon
50g pistachios, chopped
50g breadcrumbs
1 egg
50ml yoghurt
parsley and mint, to garnish
sea salt and black pepper

Tabbouleh
1 red onion, very finely chopped
50g fine bulgur wheat, washed
½ cucumber, deseeded and
    finely chopped
2 tomatoes, deseeded and
    finely chopped
large bunch of parsley, very
    finely chopped
small bunch of dill,
    very finely chopped
small bunch of mint, leaves
    only, very finely chopped
1 tbsp olive oil
juice of 1 lime

Dressing
100ml yoghurt
juice of 1 lime
1 tbsp tahini
½ tsp honey
¼ tsp each of ground allspice,
    cinnamon and cardamom

There's a nice Iranian vibe to these fabulously fruity meatballs. The addition of the dried cherries and pistachios turn humble lamb mince into a superstar, and if you fancy a bit more heat, chuck in some chilli flakes. Serve with a herby tabbouleh salad.

Put the red onion for the tabbouleh in a bowl, season with salt and cover with cold water. Leave for half an hour while you make the meatballs. Put the dried cherries for the meatballs in a bowl of hot water and leave them to soak too.

Preheat the oven to 200°C/Fan 180°C/Gas 6. Put the lamb mince in a bowl. Drain the cherries and roughly chop them, then add them to the bowl with all the other meatball ingredients and season well. Mix thoroughly – the easiest way to make sure everything is well combined is to knead the mixture with your hands. Divide the mixture into 20 balls and place them on a baking tray. Bake them in the oven for about 15 minutes until lightly browned. The meatballs may be slightly pink inside, but that's good – you don't want to overcook them.

While the meatballs are in the oven, make the tabbouleh. Rinse the bulgur wheat in cold water until it runs clear, then drain it and put it in a salad bowl. Drain the red onion and add it to the bulgur, then add all the remaining vegetables and herbs. Season with salt and pepper and drizzle over the olive oil and lemon juice, then toss to combine.

To make the dressing for the meatballs, mix everything together with plenty of seasoning. Serve the meatballs with the tabbouleh and dressing and garnish with parsley and mint.

CHILLI CON CARNE WITH CORN TOPPING

SERVES 4 | PREP: 20 MINS | COOK: ABOUT 1¾ HOURS

This has all the comforting qualities of a shepherd's pie – but with a difference. Our tasty beef chilli has a traditional Mexican topping of sweetcorn and jalapeños and is creamy, spicy and totally fab. Dig in and enjoy.

2 tbsp olive oil
1 red onion, diced
1 red pepper, diced
100g smoked bacon lardons
500g beef mince
4 garlic cloves, finely
    chopped
1 tbsp ground cumin
1 tsp ground cinnamon
1 tbsp chipotle paste
1 tbsp ground oregano
400g can of chopped
    tomatoes
2 x 400g cans of beans
    (pinto, red kidney or
    black), drained
400ml stock or water
sea salt and black pepper

Topping
400g frozen sweetcorn
    kernels
50g butter
1 tbsp cornflour
1 tsp baking powder
2 tbsp chopped pickled
    jalapeños (optional)
small bunch of coriander
100g Cheddar cheese,
    grated

Heat the oil in a large flameproof casserole dish and add the onion and red pepper. Sauté over a medium heat until the onion is soft and translucent, then turn up the heat and add the bacon. Cook, stirring regularly, until the bacon is crisp, then add the beef mince. Continue to cook, stirring at intervals, until the beef is nicely browned.

Add the garlic, spices, chipotle paste and oregano and season with plenty of salt and pepper. Stir for a minute or so, then add the tomatoes, beans and stock or water. Bring to the boil, then turn down the heat and cover the dish. Leave to simmer for an hour, stirring regularly.

Preheat the oven to 180°C/Fan 160°C/Gas 4. To make the topping, put half the sweetcorn kernels in a food processor with the butter, cornflour and baking powder. Blitz until smooth. Season with salt and pepper, then add the rest of the corn. Process again until you have a textured mixture with a dropping consistency. Season with plenty of salt and pepper and stir through the jalapeños, if using.

Roughly chop the coriander and sprinkle it over the chilli. Spoon the corn mixture on top, smoothing it out carefully and making sure it completely covers the chilli. Sprinkle with the grated cheese. Bake in the oven for about 30 minutes until the top is a deep golden brown.

HAWAIIAN MEATBALL POKE BOWL

SERVES 4 | PREP: 20 MINS (PLUS SALTING TIME) | COOK: 15 MINS (PLUS RICE COOKING TIME)

Meatballs
300g pork mince
3 or 4 spring onions,
    finely chopped
15g root ginger, grated
2 garlic cloves, crushed
1 tsp Chinese five-spice
    powder
50g breadcrumbs
1 egg
sea salt and black pepper

Salsa
150g cucumber, diced
150g watermelon, diced
100g pineapple, diced
1 small red onion, finely
    chopped
1 tbsp lime juice
½ tsp chilli flakes
small bunch of mint,
    leaves only

To assemble
200g red cabbage,
    finely shredded
150g brown rice
watercress or other
    mustardy green leaves,
    leafy tips only
sesame oil
soy sauce
sesame seeds, to garnish
herbs (microherbs, mint,
    coriander), to garnish

Lots of ingredients, yes, but this is mostly an assembly job and fun to eat. The poke bowl was our first inspiration for the dish, then we put that idea together with our love of meatballs and Si's mission to put pineapple with everything and came up with this! It's a festival of taste and texture – and a bit healthy too.

First make the meatballs. Preheat the oven to 200°C/Fan 180°C/Gas 6. Mix all the meatball ingredients together and add plenty of seasoning. Shape the mixture into about 16 balls and place them on a baking tray. Bake for about 15 minutes until piping hot and browned. The meatballs can also be shallow fried in oil if you prefer. Keep them warm while you prepare the other elements.

Make the salsa by mixing everything together in a bowl and seasoning with salt and black pepper.

Put the cabbage in a sieve or colander and sprinkle with salt. Leave to stand for half an hour. Cook the brown rice according to the packet instructions or use our recipe on page 262.

To assemble, divide the rice, meatballs, cabbage, salsa and watercress between 4 bowls. Drizzle with sesame oil and soy sauce, then sprinkle with sesame seeds and herbs. Take the sesame oil and soy sauce to the table so everyone can add more if they like.

VEGGIE

CARIBBEAN CHICKPEA & SPINACH CURRY

SERVES 4 | PREP: 15 MINS | COOK: ABOUT 35 MINS

To all you curry lovers out there – try a Caribbean recipe for a change. This is a proper tasty, satisfying vegetable curry and it happens to be fine for vegans too. You can buy plantains in the supermarket. Look for ones that are semi-ripe – turning yellow, but not brown spotted. Very green plantains are a bit too starchy for this recipe and ripe ones are too sweet.

1 tbsp coconut oil

1 onion, sliced in thin wedges

3 garlic cloves, finely chopped

250g pumpkin or squash, diced

1 tbsp Caribbean curry powder (see p.260 or shop-bought)

1 scotch bonnet or 1–2 tsp scotch bonnet hot sauce

1 large thyme sprig

400ml can of coconut milk

2 x 400g cans of chickpeas, drained

250g frozen spinach (whole leaf, no need to defrost)

salt and black pepper

Plantain

1 large, semi-ripe plantain

zest and juice of 1 lime

½ tsp Caribbean curry powder

1 tbsp coconut oil

To garnish

2 spring onions, finely sliced (include the greens)

squeeze of lime juice

Heat the coconut oil in a large saucepan or a flameproof casserole dish. Add the onion and sauté over a medium-high heat for a few minutes until it starts to brown. Add the garlic and pumpkin or squash and stir for another couple of minutes.

Add the curry powder and stir to coat the vegetables. If using the scotch bonnet, pierce it with a knife and add it, whole, to the saucepan along with the thyme. Pour over the coconut milk and stir to make sure the base of the saucepan is completely deglazed and you've scraped up all the sticky bits, then add the chickpeas and frozen spinach. Season with salt and pepper. If using hot sauce, stir it in at this point, adding a teaspoon at a time until you get the amount of heat you want.

Bring to the boil, then turn the heat down and partially cover the pan. Simmer for 15–20 minutes until the squash is tender and the sauce is slightly reduced.

While the curry is simmering, prepare the plantain. Peel and slice it on the diagonal, then toss it in the lime zest, juice and curry powder and season with salt. Heat the coconut oil and fry the plantain on both sides until well browned.

Fish out the scotch bonnet, if using, and serve the curry garnished with the plantain, finely sliced spring onions and a squeeze of lime juice.

HALLOUMI BURGERS

SERVES 4 | PREP: 10 MINS (PLUS STRAINING TIME) | COOK: 10 MINS

Like many people, we're eating more halloumi these days and it's a really useful veggie option. It makes a great meat-free burger and it tastes the business served with the chilli jam and yoghurt dressing. A plate full of flavour and texture.

2 blocks of halloumi cheese
2 tbsp olive oil
juice of 1 lemon
1 tsp dried oregano
sea salt and black pepper

Yoghurt dressing
200g Greek yoghurt
1 tsp dried mint
½ tsp dried oregano
pinch of sugar

To serve
4 ciabatta buns, split
4 large lettuce leaves
4 tbsp chilli jam
4 slices of red onion
4 rings of green pepper
8 slices of cucumber,
   cut on the diagonal
mint leaves

First make the yoghurt dressing. Strain the yoghurt through a muslin-lined sieve for half an hour to drain off any excess liquid, then mix with the herbs, sugar and plenty of seasoning. Set aside.

Cut each block of cheese into 4 thick slices. Whisk the olive oil and lemon juice with half a teaspoon of salt and the oregano. Pour this over the cheese slices and turn so they are completely coated. Heat a griddle pan or frying pan and add the cheese. Grill for 2–3 minutes on each side until charred or well browned.

To assemble, lightly toast the ciabatta buns. Add a dollop of the yoghurt dressing to the bottom half of each ciabatta bun, then top with a lettuce leaf. Add a slice of halloumi, a tablespoon of chilli jam and a slice of red onion. Add the second slice of halloumi, top with green pepper, 2 cucumber slices and some mint, then add a little more yoghurt dressing. Sandwich with the top halves of the ciabatta buns. Serve immediately.

FRYING PAN PIZZAS

SERVES 4 | PREP: 15 MINS (PLUS PROVING TIME) | COOK: ABOUT 35 MINS

Don't despair if you don't have a fancy pizza oven. You can cook this quick and easy pizza in a frying pan and you get a lovely crunchy crust. Our special dough doesn't have to be kneaded, so saves on elbow grease, but it does need a long rise. You can make the dough well in advance, though, and once it has risen each pizza is ready in a matter of minutes.

Dough
500g plain flour (preferably 00 pasta flour)
5g instant yeast
1 tsp sugar
1 tsp salt
2 tbsp olive oil, plus extra for greasing
300ml tepid water

Topping
2 tbsp olive oil
400g mushrooms (any type), sliced
½ tsp dried oregano
3 garlic cloves, crushed
thyme sprig tips
200g Taleggio cheese
1 ball of mozzarella
sea salt and black pepper

To serve
handful of rocket or watercress
olive oil, for drizzling

To make the dough, put the flour into a bowl and mix in the yeast, sugar and salt. Mix the olive oil into the tepid water, then gradually add this to the flour until you have a slightly sticky, smooth dough. Oil a large food bag or lidded plastic container and add the dough. Seal and leave in the fridge for at least 24 hours or up to 3 days. You can also freeze the dough at this point.

Remove the dough from the fridge, cut it into 4 pieces and shape them into balls. Cover with a damp cloth and leave to double in size – this will take up to 2 hours.

Now make the mushroom topping. Heat the oil in a frying pan and add the mushrooms. Fry briskly, stirring regularly, until well browned, then season with salt and pepper and stir in the oregano, garlic and some of the thyme. Cook for another 2–3 minutes. Prepare the cheeses by roughly tearing or slicing them and set them aside.

Preheat the grill and at the same time heat an ovenproof frying pan or cast-iron skillet on the hob until hot.

Working quickly, take the first ball of dough and stretch it into a round which will fit snugly into your frying pan. Arrange the dough in the pan, then cook until the underside is browned – this will probably take 3–4 minutes, Then add a quarter of the cheeses, followed by a quarter of the mushrooms and a few more sprigs of thyme.

Put the pizza under the grill until the cheese has melted and is lightly browned. Add a few rocket leaves or sprigs of watercress. Drizzle with olive oil and repeat until all 4 pizzas are made.

PIZZA PIE

SERVES 4 | PREP: 10 MINS | COOK: 40 MINS

Another triumph for frozen puff pastry, this cross between a pizza and a pie is super-easy to make and looks stunning. It's great with just the classic topping of tomato sauce, mozzarella and basil, but feel free to add pepperoni or whatever else you like. This makes a good supper with some salad or you can cut the pie up into little slices and serve it as a snack with drinks.

Pizza sauce
1 tbsp olive oil
400g can of chopped
   tomatoes
1 tbsp tomato purée
½ tsp dried oregano
2 garlic cloves, crushed
   or grated
1 tsp red wine vinegar
a couple of large basil stems
pinch of sugar, if needed
salt and black pepper

To assemble
1 pack of ready-rolled
   puff pastry
1 large ball of mozzarella
a few basil leaves
a drizzle of olive oil

First make the pizza sauce. Put all the ingredients, except the sugar, into a saucepan with plenty of salt and pepper. Bring to the boil, then turn the heat down and simmer until the tomatoes have reduced to a thick, jammy consistency. Taste and add a pinch of sugar if necessary and adjust the seasoning. Remove the basil stems and leave to cool.

When you are ready to bake your pizza, preheat the oven to 220°C/Fan 200°C/Gas 7. Unroll the pastry on to a baking tray and score a 1cm border all the way around. Spread the tomato sauce inside the border, then tear up the mozzarella and arrange the pieces over the sauce. Sprinkle over a few basil leaves and drizzle with olive oil. Brush the border of pastry with olive oil too.

Bake in the preheated oven for 15–20 minutes until the pastry is cooked through and is turning gold and the cheese has melted and started to brown. Serve at once.

CHILLI BEAN BURGERS

SERVES 4 | PREP: 20 MINS (PLUS COOLING AND CHILLING TIME) | COOK: 25 MINS

If you're a burgerholic like we are, you're always on the lookout for something new. Here's our latest incarnation of the veggie burger which has bags of flavour and a nice hit of chilli. Good served Mexican style with avocado and a dash of soured cream. A complete meal.

2-3 tbsp olive oil
1 small onion, very finely chopped
½ red pepper, very finely chopped
1 small carrot, finely grated
2 jalapeños, very finely chopped (include seeds)
3 tbsp coriander stems, finely chopped
4 garlic cloves, finely chopped
1-2 tsp chilli paste or hot sauce (such as chipotle)
1 tbsp soy sauce
1 tsp ground cumin
½ tsp ground cinnamon
400g can of black, pinto or kidney beans, drained
50g cooked brown rice
75g breadcrumbs
1 egg
sea salt and black pepper

To serve
1 avocado
juice of 1 lime
cheese slices (optional)
4 burger buns
4 lettuce leaves
4 slices of red onion
soured cream (optional)
coriander leaves, to garnish
hot sauce

Heat a tablespoon of oil in a frying pan. Add the onion, red pepper and carrot and cook until the onion is soft and translucent and the vegetables are collapsed down and glossy, but dry. Add the jalapeños, coriander stems and garlic and stir for another couple of minutes. Stir in the chilli paste or hot sauce, soy sauce, cumin and cinnamon and season with salt and pepper. Set aside to cool.

Put the beans into a bowl and mash them roughly – you want a mixture of textures. Add the rice, breadcrumbs, egg and the cooled vegetables. Season with more salt and pepper and mix thoroughly.

Heat a little more oil in the frying pan, take a dessertspoonful of the mixture and form it into a small patty. Fry briefly on both sides and taste for heat and seasoning. Add more salt, pepper or chilli to the main mixture if necessary. When you are satisfied with the flavour, form the mixture into 4 patties and chill them for at least an hour – this will help the flavour develop.

When you are ready to eat, remove the patties from the fridge. Peel the avocado, remove the stone and slice the flesh. Toss the slices in the lime juice and season with salt.

Heat more oil in a frying pan and add the patties. Cook over a medium heat until a brown crust forms underneath and the patties come away from the pan with ease. Carefully flip the burgers to fry the other side. If serving with cheese, add it to the burgers now and put something over the pan to help the cheese melt – a lid partially covering the pan is fine.

Lightly toast the burger buns, then layer up the lettuce leaves, onion, avocado slices, burgers, cheese, if using, and soured cream, if you like. Garnish with coriander leaves and serve with extra hot sauce.

VEGGIE CHILLI BURRITOS

SERVES 4 | PREP: 20 MINS | COOK: 40 MINS

2 tbsp olive oil

1 onion, finely chopped

1 green or red pepper,
  finely chopped

2 celery sticks, finely
  chopped

4 garlic cloves, finely
  chopped

3 jalapeños or 1 scotch
  bonnet or habanero,
  finely chopped

1 tbsp ancho chilli flakes

1 tsp chipotle paste

1 tbsp ground cumin

1 tbsp fresh oregano, finely
  chopped

200g fresh tomatoes, puréed

1 x 400g can each of black
  beans, kidney beans and
  pinto beans

sea salt and black pepper

Rice

100g long-grain rice, rinsed

zest of 1 lime

stems from a small bunch of
  coriander, finely chopped

Serving options

4 large tortillas

guacamole (see p.266
  or shop-bought)

tomato salsa (see p.266
  or shop-bought)

soured cream

Cheddar cheese, grated

coriander, chopped

pickled jalapeños

The chilli mixture actually makes more than you need for four burritos, but we think it's worth making the whole lot – it's so good. You can freeze some to serve as a chilli with rice on another day or just invite people round and make more burritos. The chilli keeps for a week in the fridge.

First make the bean chilli. Heat the oil in a large pan or a flameproof casserole dish and add the onion, pepper and celery. Cook until soft and translucent, then add the garlic and chillies. Continue to cook for another couple of minutes.

Stir in the chilli flakes, chipotle paste, cumin, oregano, tomatoes and beans. Season with salt and pepper and add 100ml of water.

Bring to the boil, then turn the heat down to a simmer and leave to cook, uncovered, for 15-20 minutes until the sauce has reduced down. Stir regularly to make sure it isn't catching on the bottom. The consistency should be quite thick, if not dry.

To cook the rice, put it in a pan with the lime zest, coriander stems and 150ml of water. Season with salt, bring to the boil and cover. Turn down the heat and simmer for about 15 minutes until all the water has been absorbed. Take the pan off the heat and remove the lid. Put a tea towel over the top of the pan and place the lid on top. Leave the rice to steam in its own heat for a further 10 minutes.

To assemble, heat each tortilla on a dry frying pan for just a few seconds on each side to make them easier to fold. Spoon the chilli into the centre of the tortillas in a roughly rectangular shape and add the rice and as many of the serving options as you want. Fold over the sides, then fold over one of the remaining edges and roll. Wrap the burritos in foil to make them easier to hold while eating.

SPINACH & LENTIL PIE

SERVES 4 | PREP: 20 MINS (PLUS CHILLING TIME) | COOK: 40 MINS

This makes an excellent veggie supper. There's protein, carbs and plenty of veg, so the pie is a meal in itself, although a tomato salad might be nice on the side. If you're short of time you could use ready-made pastry and we won't tell on you.

2 tbsp olive oil

1 bunch of spring onions, sliced

1 courgette, coarsely grated

1 garlic clove

zest and juice of 1 lemon

400g can of lentils, drained

500g frozen spinach, defrosted and drained

250g feta cheese, crumbled

½ tsp cinnamon

sea salt and black pepper

Pastry

300g plain flour

½ tsp salt

150g butter, chilled and diced

1 egg

1–2 tbsp iced water

1 egg, beaten with 1 tbsp of water

First make the pastry. Put the flour into a bowl with half a teaspoon of salt and add the butter. Rub the butter in until the mixture resembles breadcrumbs, then mix in the egg. Add just enough iced water to bind the mixture. Form into a ball of dough, then wrap in cling film and chill for at least an hour.

To make the filling, heat the olive oil in a large sauté pan. Add the spring onions and courgette. Cook until the courgette has collapsed down, then stir in the rest of the ingredients and season with salt and pepper. Leave to cool.

Preheat the oven to 200°C/Fan 180°C/Gas 6. Roll out about two-thirds of the dough to line a deep pie dish (we used one measuring about 26 x 19cm), then pile in the filling. Brush the edges of the pastry with beaten egg, then roll out the remaining dough and place it on top. Seal and crimp the edges of the pie, then brush the top with beaten egg.

Bake in the preheated oven for about 30 minutes until the pastry is beautifully crisp and golden.

PINTO BEAN CASSEROLE

SERVES 4 | PREP: 15 MINS | COOK: ABOUT 30 MINS

This is based on a wonderful Iranian bean dish called loobia chiti, which can be served as an appetiser, as part of a meze selection or a main dish. We've added extra greens to our version to make a good substantial veggie/vegan supper. Nice with flatbread.

2 tbsp olive oil

1 large onion, diced

2 courgettes, diced

3 garlic cloves, finely
    chopped

zest of 1 lemon

2 bay leaves

1 tsp cumin seeds

1 tsp turmeric

1 tsp hot paprika

300g fresh ripe tomatoes,
    puréed

2 x 400g cans of pinto beans,
    drained

200g frozen spinach cubes

salt and black pepper

To serve

leaves from a small bunch
    of mint

leaves from a small bunch
    of parsley

lemon juice

1–2 tsp sumac

flatbread (optional)

Heat the olive oil in a large saucepan or a flameproof casserole dish. Add the onion and courgettes and cook until the onion is soft and translucent. Add the garlic, lemon zest, bay leaves and spices and stir for a couple of minutes to coat the vegetables. Pour in the tomatoes, then stir in the pinto beans and spinach cubes. Season with salt and pepper, then pour in 200ml of water.

Bring to the boil, then cover, turn the heat down to a simmer and leave to cook for 20 minutes.

Stir in some of the mint and parsley, reserving a few leaves for a garnish, then add a squeeze of lemon. Sprinkle in half the sumac and stir. Taste and adjust the sourness by adding more lemon juice to taste. Serve garnished with more herbs and sumac and maybe some flatbread on the side.

CAULIFLOWER & QUINOA BAKE

SERVES 4 | PREP: 15 MINS | COOK: ABOUT 1 HOUR

Quinoa is a superfood. It's a seed, not a grain, so can be enjoyed by those who want to avoid gluten and it's a complete protein. Here we lace it with parsley and lime zest to make a tasty topping for this veggie bake. This is another good vegan dish and nice served with greens.

1 tbsp coconut or
    vegetable oil
2 red onions, cut into wedges
300g carrots, cut into
    chunks
1 small cauliflower (about
    500g), cut into florets
3 garlic cloves, finely
    chopped
1 tbsp mild curry powder
300ml vegetable stock
400g can of chopped
    tomatoes
2 tbsp nut butter (peanut,
    almond or cashew)
salt and black pepper

Quinoa
125g quinoa
1 tbsp coconut oil
zest of 1 lime
small bunch of parsley,
    finely chopped

Heat the oil in a flameproof casserole dish and add the onions, carrots and cauliflower. Fry over a high heat for 3-4 minutes, until they start to take on some colour, then add the garlic cloves and curry powder. Season with salt and pepper, then pour in the stock.

Bring to the boil and simmer for 5 minutes, then add the tomatoes. Continue to simmer for another 10-15 minutes until the vegetable are tender and the sauce has reduced down. Gently stir in the nut butter and simmer for another couple of minutes.

While the vegetables are cooking, prepare the quinoa. Rinse and soak it in cold water for 5 minutes, then drain it thoroughly. Heat a teaspoon of the coconut oil in a saucepan and add the quinoa. Toast for a few minutes until aromatic, then add 250ml of water. Bring to the boil, then turn down the heat and cover. Simmer for about 15 minutes until all the water has been absorbed and the quinoa is tender. Preheat the oven to 200°C/Fan 180°C/Gas 6.

Stir the lime zest and parsley into the quinoa and spoon it over the vegetables. Melt the remaining coconut oil and drizzle it over the top. Bake in the oven for 20-25 minutes until the quinoa has darkened and crisped up slightly.

VEGETARIAN COTTAGE PIE

SERVES 4 | PREP: 20 MINS | COOK: ABOUT 1½ HOURS

2 tbsp olive oil
1 large onion, finely chopped
1 large carrot, finely diced
1 celery stick, finely diced
150g celeriac, parsnip or
    swede (or a combination),
    finely diced
200g mushrooms (any sort),
    finely chopped
3 garlic cloves, finely
    chopped
1 large thyme sprig
2 bay leaves
200g cooked brown lentils
2 tbsp tomato purée
100ml red wine
400ml vegetable stock
sea salt and black pepper

Colcannon topping

1kg floury potatoes, cut into
    chunks
½ green or savoy cabbage,
    shredded
50g butter, plus extra for
    dotting on top
100ml single cream
100g Cheddar cheese, grated
    (optional)

Cauliflower cheese topping

1 large cauliflower
15g butter
100g Cheddar cheese, grated

Not only is this a cracking veggie cottage pie but there's a choice of three top toppings. How's that for great value? Depending on your mood and your taste buds, choose from colcannon, cauli cheese or a three-root mash topping. All are bang on.

First make the filling. Heat the oil in a large saucepan and add the onion, carrot, celery, root veg and mushrooms. Sauté over a medium–high heat until they start to soften. The mushrooms will give out liquid during this process but once they are dry and well browned, add the garlic and cook for another couple of minutes.

Add the herbs, lentils and tomato purée and continue to cook for a couple of minutes, stirring, until everything is well coated with the purée and has a rich aroma. Pour in the wine and bring to the boil, then cook until reduced by half. Add the stock, season well, then bring to the boil again and turn down the heat. Partially cover the pan and simmer for about 30 minutes until the sauce is thick and reduced. Remove the herbs. Preheat the oven to 200°C/Fan 180°C/Gas 6.

Put the filling in a large, shallow ovenproof dish. Arrange your chosen topping over the filling as evenly as you can, making sure there are no gaps, then rough up the surface with a fork. Bake for about 30 minutes until browned and piping hot.

Colcannon topping

Bring a large pan of water to the boil and add the potatoes. Add salt, then simmer for 10-15 minutes until tender. Drain thoroughly. Wash the cabbage well. Melt half the butter in a pan and add the cabbage, then season and stir to coat with the butter. Add a splash of water and cover the pan. Cook for about 5 minutes, stirring every so often, until the cabbage is knife tender. Mash the potatoes with the remaining butter and the cream, stir in the cabbage and use to top the filling.

Cauliflower cheese topping

Bring a large pan of water to the boil. Break the cauliflower into large florets and slice the core and any edible leaves. Add a teaspoon of salt to the water, then add the cauliflower. Cook for about 5 minutes until just tender. Drain thoroughly and toss it in the butter. Roughly chop or slice and use to cover the shepherd's pie filling. Sprinkle with cheese.

Three-root mash topping
500g floury potatoes
250g celeriac
250g sweet potatoes
25g butter
50ml milk
1 tbsp wholegrain mustard

Three-root mash
Cut the floury potatoes and celeriac into 3cm dice and the sweet potatoes into 5cm dice. Celeriac and sweet potatoes get waterlogged very easily, so it's best to steam them. Bring a pan of water to the boil. Attach a steamer basket and layer up the vegetables - first the floury potatoes, then the celeriac, topped by the sweet potatoes. Season with salt and pepper as you go. Steam for 20-25 minutes until tender. Transfer to a bowl and add the butter, milk and mustard, then mash well. Use to top the filling.

SCANDINAVIAN HASH WITH MUSHROOM GRAVY

SERVES 4 | PREP: 20 MINS | COOK: ABOUT 45 MINS

We cooked a meat version of this by a lake on a Finnish archipelago some years back and thought that with a few tweaks it would make a great veggie meal. It's good for brunch or any time of day and if you want a vegan dish, just leave out the eggs, yoghurt and crème fraiche and use a little more oil instead of the butter.

300g potatoes, unpeeled
   and diced
200g carrots, diced
4 tbsp olive oil
1 large onion, diced
300g mushrooms, roughly
   chopped
15g dried mushrooms,
   soaked in 50ml warm
   water
1 tsp juniper berries, crushed
a few rasps of nutmeg
sea salt and black pepper

Mushroom gravy
1 tbsp olive oil
25g butter
1 shallot, finely chopped
200g mushrooms, very
   finely chopped
1 thyme sprig
1 tbsp plain flour
250ml mushroom stock
1 tbsp mushroom ketchup
100g yoghurt or crème
   fraiche (optional)

To serve
4 fried eggs
lingonberry jam (optional)

Bring a saucepan of water to the boil. Add the potatoes and carrots and boil for 5 minutes, then drain thoroughly.

Heat 3 tablespoons of the olive oil in a large, preferably non-stick or cast-iron frying pan. Add the onion, potatoes and carrots and fry, turning regularly, until everything is brown and crisp. This will take about 15 minutes.

In a separate pan, heat the remaining oil and add the chopped mushrooms. Fry until well browned and dry, then fold them into the potato mixture. Drain the dried mushrooms and chop them finely, reserving the soaking water. Add them to the potatoes along with the juniper berries. Season with plenty of salt and pepper and nutmeg. Strain the mushroom soaking water and pour this over too. Continue to cook for a few more minutes, stirring regularly.

To make the gravy, heat the olive oil and butter together in a saucepan. Add the shallot and cook until soft and translucent. Add the mushrooms and cook until dry. Stir in the thyme and season with salt and pepper. Stir in the flour and cook for a couple of minutes until the mixture no longer looks floury. Add a splash of the stock and stir as it thickens to a roux, then gradually work in the rest of the stock and the mushroom ketchup. You will end up with a thin gravy. Stir through the yoghurt or crème fraiche, if using, and heat through.

Serve the hash with the mushroom gravy, fried eggs and perhaps some lingonberry jam on the side.

PUDDINGS
& TARTS

APPLE & CHERRY CRUMBLE

SERVES 4 | PREP: 20 MINS | COOK: 35-40 MINS

Turns out that a good old crumble is a top favourite with many people – including us. Cherries and almonds are a match made in heaven, so we've added cherries to the trad apples for the filling and included ground almonds, plus some flaked almonds in the topping, if you like. Frozen cherries are fine and we find that as much as we love Bramleys, using eating apples means you need less sugar in the filling. If you like a bit more crunch, add a couple of tablespoons of oats to the topping mix. A great one for the crumble repertoire.

Filling
400g cherries, pitted
3 eating apples, peeled,
    cored and chopped
1 tbsp cornflour
1 tbsp caster sugar
1 tbsp cherry liqueur
    or Kirsch (optional)

Topping
100g plain flour
50g ground almonds
pinch of salt
125g butter, softened
50g flaked almonds
    (optional)
35g demerara sugar

To serve
cream or custard

Preheat the oven to 200°C/Fan 180°C/Gas 6.

Put the cherries and apples in an ovenproof dish and sprinkle over the cornflour. Mix thoroughly, making sure there are no lumps or flecks of cornflour, then stir in the caster sugar and the cherry liqueur or Kirsch, if using.

To make the topping, put the flour and ground almonds in a bowl with a generous pinch of salt. Add the butter and rub it in until the mixture is clumpy. Stir in the flaked almonds, if using, and the sugar. Sprinkle the topping over the fruit.

Bake in the preheated oven for 35-40 minutes until the top is golden and some of the juice from the fruit is starting to break through. Serve with cream or custard.

CRANACHAN RICE PUDDING

SERVES 4 | PREP: 10 MINS | COOK: 45 MINS

The Scots love cranachan; the English love rice pudding. Here we have created a magical union of the two that's great served hot or cold. We like to serve it with some caraway and lemon shortbread (page 246) on the side. Or for a posh dinner party, try layering the rice pud, then berries and oat topping in little jars. Very impressive.

200g pudding/short-grain
    rice
50g caster sugar
1.25 litres whole milk
pinch of salt
2 tbsp honey
1 tbsp whisky (or more
    to taste)

Oat topping
25g honey
35g maple syrup
25g butter
1 tbsp whisky
60g oats
large pinch of salt

To finish
300g blueberries
1 tbsp caster sugar

Put the rice, sugar and milk in a saucepan with a generous pinch of salt. Bring to the boil, then turn the heat down and simmer gently for 20–25 minutes until the rice is cooked through and the milk has thickened into the consistency of a sauce. Stir regularly to prevent the rice from catching on the bottom. Stir in the honey and whisky.

Preheat the oven to 180°C/Fan 160°C/Gas 4. To make the oat topping, put the honey, maple syrup and butter in a small saucepan and heat until the butter has melted. Stir in the whisky, followed by the oats and a large pinch of salt, then stir until the oats are completely coated. Put a piece of baking parchment on a baking tray and spread the mixture out. Bake for about 15 minutes, stirring regularly, until the oats are lightly toasted. Remove from the oven and cool.

Put half the blueberries in a saucepan with the sugar and a splash of water. Heat until the sugar has dissolved and the blueberries have started to bleed and thicken into a sauce. Remove from the heat. When the mixture has cooled down, add the remaining blueberries and shake the saucepan just to coat the blueberries in the juice.

Serve the rice pudding with spoonfuls of blueberries and a sprinkling of the oat mixture on top.

PINEAPPLE & RUM STICKY TOFFEE PUDDING

SERVES 4-6 | PREP: 20 MINS | COOK: 30-35 MINS

Sticky toffee pud meets a cocktail and the result is fabulous. We hope you'll enjoy our new take on an old favourite. Don't use a loose-bottomed tin, though, and make sure the baking parchment liner is completely sealed, otherwise the butter/sugar mix will leak through.

Base/topping
50g butter, softened
25g soft light brown sugar
25g soft dark brown sugar
1 large can of pineapple rings

Sponge
200g medjool dates
175ml just-boiled water
25ml rum
1 tsp bicarbonate of soda
175g self-raising flour
½ tsp salt
85g butter, softened
75g soft light brown sugar
75g soft dark brown sugar
1 tbsp treacle
2 eggs, beaten
100ml milk (or use pineapple
    juice from the can)
50g crystallised pineapple,
    chopped (optional)

Rum butterscotch sauce
175g soft dark brown sugar
50g butter
200ml double cream
1-2 tbsp rum, to taste

To serve (optional)
cream or ice cream

Preheat the oven to 180°C/Fan 160°C/Gas 4. Line a square brownie tin with some baking parchment or a liner. Rub the butter over the lined base of the tin. Mix the sugars together and sprinkle them over the butter. Arrange the pineapple over the top and set aside.

Finely chop the dates and cover them with the boiled water and the rum. Add the bicarbonate of soda and leave to stand until the dates have swollen and softened and the liquid is thick.

Mix the flour and salt together. Beat the butter, sugars and treacle together until very soft and aerated, then add the flour and eggs. Pour in the milk or pineapple juice and mix briefly, then stir in the dates including their soaking liquid. Stir in the crystallised pineapple, if using.

Pour the sponge mixture over the pineapple, then bake in the oven for 30-35 minutes until well risen and springy to the touch. Turn out on to a large serving plate and remove the baking paper – it should look a bit like a dark pineapple upside-down pudding.

While the pudding is baking, make the sauce. Melt the sugar, butter and half the cream in a small pan, stirring until the sugar has completely dissolved. Slowly bring to the boil and let it bubble for a couple of minutes, then remove the pan from the heat. Add the remaining cream and the rum and stir to combine. Transfer to a jug.

Serve the pudding with the sauce poured over and some extra cream or ice cream, if you like.

ELVIS BREAD & BUTTER PUDDING

SERVES 4 | PREP: 15 MINS (PLUS STANDING TIME) | COOK: 35–40 MINS

We do believe Elvis would have loved this extra-special bread and butter pud which contains two of his favourite things – chocolate and bananas – so put on your blue suede shoes and knock out this tribute to the king. And if you really want to go OTT, you could add some peanut butter too. Use an ordinary sandwich loaf or some brioche, if you like.

butter, softened, for
   spreading, plus extra
   for greasing
5–6 slices of white bread
2 bananas, sliced
50g chocolate chips
   (milk or dark)
zest of 1 lime
50g caster sugar
2 eggs
200ml double cream
150ml milk
25ml rum
1–2 tbsp demerara sugar

Butter a deep ovenproof dish. Cut the crusts off the bread or leave them on if you prefer, then butter the slices and cut them in half on the diagonal. Arrange half the slices over the base of the dish, buttered-side up.

Sprinkle over half the banana slices and half the chocolate chips. Sprinkle over half the lime zest. Repeat these layers – bread, banana, chocolate chips and zest.

Whisk the sugar and eggs together until smooth, then stir in the cream, milk and rum. Pour this mixture over the contents of the dish, pressing down the bread lightly. Leave to stand for half an hour.

Preheat the oven to 180°C/Fan 160°C/Gas 4. Place the dish on a baking tray. Sprinkle the top of the pudding with demerara sugar, making sure all the bananas are covered with it, then bake in the oven for 35–40 minutes until the custard has set and slightly puffed up and the top is lightly browned. Remove from the oven and leave to stand for 10 minutes before serving. Great hot or cold.

FIG & SHERRY ETON MESS

SERVES 4 | PREP: 25 MINS | COOK: 1½–2 HOURS

We've always thought that Eton mess was the pud you make when your pavlova goes wrong. But it's well worth messing up for this version that's dressed with figs, sherry and a dash of orange zest and honey. A lovely dessert and it looks a bit smart if you want to show off.

Meringues
50g blanched hazelnuts
2 egg whites
125g caster sugar
pinch of salt

Figs
8–12 figs depending on size,
    trimmed and halved
1–2 tbsp honey
1 tsp orange zest
pinch of salt
50ml sherry, such as Oloroso

Cream
200g double or whipping
    cream
200g Greek yoghurt
1 tbsp icing sugar

To serve
mint leaves
orange zest, grated

First make the meringues. Preheat the oven to 120°C/Fan 100°C/Gas ½ and line a baking tray with baking parchment. Put the hazelnuts in a dry frying pan and toast them over a medium heat, shaking the pan regularly, until they are a very light brown. Remove and allow to cool, then chop very finely in a food processor. It's best to use the pulse button to make sure you don't chop them too much – if you overgrind the nuts, they will start releasing their oil.

Whisk the egg whites to stiff peaks, then add a third of the sugar. Whisk again and gradually add the rest of the sugar until the meringue is very stiff and glossy. Fold in the hazelnuts with a pinch of salt.

Dollop the meringue mixture in large mounds over the baking tray. Bake in the oven for 1–1½ hours until the meringues are crisp and cracking round the edges. Lift the meringues off the paper and check their bottoms. If they're not quite ready, turn them upside down and leave them in the oven for another 15 minutes to dry out. Leave to cool.

To cook the figs, preheat the oven to 200°C/Fan 180°C/Gas 6. Put the figs in a large, ovenproof dish. Drizzle over the honey and sprinkle with orange zest and a pinch of salt. Pour over the sherry. Cover the dish with foil and bake the figs in the oven for 15–20 minutes until tender. Remove from the oven and set the figs aside to cool completely.

For the cream, put the double or whipping cream into a bowl and whisk until it starts to thicken, then add the yoghurt and icing sugar.

To assemble, break up the meringues and mix with the cream and figs. Spoon over any liquid from baking the figs. Pile into bowls and garnish with mint leaves and a little more orange zest.

BAKEWELL TRIFLE

SERVES 6 | PREP: 30 MINS (PLUS CHILLING TIME) | COOK: ABOUT 45 MINS

We know you love a trifle and we know you love a Bakewell tart. We've played matchmaker and created a wonderful marriage of the two - the most beautiful trifle you will ever taste. Definitely a trifle with a twist.

Sponge
25g self-raising flour
1 tsp baking powder
85g ground almonds
pinch of salt
110g butter, softened
110g caster sugar
a few drops of almond
    extract (optional)
2 eggs, beaten
1-2 tbsp milk

Custard
250ml milk
250ml double cream
50g ground almonds
    (optional)
1 vanilla pod, split
a few drops of almond
    extract
5 egg yolks
75g caster sugar
2 tsp cornflour

To assemble
2 tbsp raspberry jam
100g amaretti biscuits
100ml Oloroso sherry or
    almond liqueur
200g raspberries
500g double cream
30g flaked almonds, toasted

Preheat the oven to 200°C/Fan 180°C/Gas 6 and line a 20cm round cake tin with baking parchment.

Mix the flour and baking powder with the ground almonds and a pinch of salt. Cream the butter and sugar with the almond extract, if using, until pale and fluffy, then incorporate the beaten eggs and the flour mixture with just enough milk to make a dropping consistency. Scrape the batter into the cake tin.

Bake in the oven for 25-30 minutes until the cake is golden brown and springy but firm to the touch. Remove from the oven and leave to stand for a few minutes before transferring to a rack to finish cooling.

To make the custard, put the milk, cream and ground almonds, if using, into a saucepan with the vanilla pod and a few drops of almond extract. Bring to just below boiling point, then remove the pan from the heat and set aside. Put the egg yolks, caster sugar and cornflour into a bowl. Whisk until the mixture is very pale and the consistency of fairly stiff foam.

Remove the vanilla pod from the milk, then pour the milk on to the egg mixture, whisking constantly until combined. Pour back into the saucepan. Cook, stirring constantly, until the custard thickens - this will happen very quickly so don't leave it unattended. Whisk until smooth, then transfer to a jug and cover with oiled cling film to stop a skin from forming - make sure the cling film is in contact with the surface of the custard. When cool, chill in the fridge.

To assemble, cut the cake in half horizontally and sandwich with the jam. Cut into chunks and arrange them over the base of your trifle bowl. Top with the amaretti, then pour over the sherry.

Add the raspberries in a single layer on top, then pour over the custard. Whip the cream until it forms soft peaks, then smooth it over the custard. Sprinkle with toasted almonds and chill for at least an hour before serving.

PASSION FRUIT & STRAWBERRY TARTLETS

MAKES 8-12 | PREP: 30 MINS (PLUS CHILLING TIME) | COOK: ABOUT 45 MINS

The delicate fragrance of passion fruit combined with luxurious crème patissière and fresh strawberries makes these dainty little tarts a real tea-time treat.

Pastry
250g plain flour, plus extra
    for dusting
1 tbsp icing sugar
pinch of salt
125g butter, chilled and diced
1 egg
iced water

Passion fruit crème patissière
100g passion fruit juice
    (strained pulp from about
    6 passion fruit)
150ml milk
3 egg yolks
75g caster sugar
15g cornflour
pinch of salt

To serve
400g strawberries, sliced
icing sugar

First make the tartlet cases. Put the flour in a bowl with the icing sugar and a pinch of salt. Rub in the butter, then mix in the egg and enough iced water to bind. Form into a dough, wrap and chill for at least an hour.

Preheat the oven to 200°C/Fan 180°C/Gas 6. Roll out the pastry on a floured work surface and cut out 12 x 7.5-8cm rounds. Use these to line a 12-hole muffin tin or alternatively, use 8-12 individual tartlet cases. Chill again for at least half an hour.

Put a circle of baking parchment in each pastry case and add baking beans. Bake in the oven for 12-15 minutes, or until you can see the pastry start to brown around the edges, then remove them from the oven. Remove the baking beans and parchment and return them to the oven for a further 10-15 minutes until the pastry is cooked. Remove the cases from the oven and leave to cool completely.

To make the crème patissière, put the strained passion fruit juice and milk into a saucepan. It might look as though it is going to curdle, but don't worry, the end result will be perfectly smooth. Warm through until the mixture is about blood temperature, then remove the pan from the heat.

Beat the egg yolks and sugar together in a bowl until pale and foamy. Beat in the cornflour with a pinch of salt. Pour the warmed passion fruit mixture into the egg yolk mixture from a height, stirring to combine, then transfer it all back to the saucepan. Stir over a gentle heat until the mixture thickens. At this point, swap a spoon for a whisk and whisk vigorously to make sure no lumps develop while the crème patissière thickens. Transfer to a container and cover with a piece of oiled cling film, making sure it is in contact with the surface area of the crème patissière. Chill thoroughly.

To assemble, divide the crème patissière between the tartlet cases and top with the strawberries. Dust with icing sugar and serve.

LEMON & BLUEBERRY PAVLOVA

SERVES 4-6 | PREP: 30 MINS (PLUS COOLING TIME) | COOK: 1½ HOURS

One of our readers' favourite desserts – and one of ours too – a pavlova is a showstopper of a pud. This lemon and blueberry version, with a hint of yuzu and tequila, is really special and well worth taking the time over. If yuzu is new to you, it's a citrus fruit that's popular in Japan and its zest and juice add a wonderful flavour to both sweet and savoury dishes. You can find it in Asian stores and supermarkets, but otherwise, just use extra lemon juice.

Meringue
6 large egg whites
300g caster sugar
1 tsp cornflour
1 tsp white wine vinegar
zest of 1 lemon

Syrup
100g granulated sugar
juice and pared zest of
   2 lemons
2 tbsp yuzu, grapefruit or
   orange juice (optional,
   add more lemon juice,
   if not using)
1 tbsp tequila (optional)

To assemble
300ml double or whipping
   cream
1 tbsp icing sugar
300g blueberries

Preheat the oven to 180°C/Fan 160°C/Gas 4. Line a baking sheet with baking parchment. Draw a 23cm round on the baking parchment to help you shape the meringue base.

Whisk the egg whites until they form soft peaks. Gradually add the sugar, a tablespoon at a time to start with, whisking vigorously in between each addition, until the meringue is stiff and glossy. Mix the cornflour and vinegar together and whisk into the meringue along with the lemon zest.

Pile the meringue on to the baking parchment, using your drawn circle for guidance. Make sure that you leave a dip in the middle of the meringue and build up the sides a bit. Place it in the oven and immediately turn the temperature down to 150°C/Fan 130°C/Gas 2. Bake for an hour, then turn off the heat, open the door and leave the pavlova to cool in the oven.

To make the syrup, put the sugar, lemon juice and lemon zest into a small pan. Slowly heat, stirring until the sugar has dissolved, then bring to the boil. Turn down to a simmer and cook until the syrup reaches the thread stage – this will take about 10 minutes and the syrup should reach a temperature of 112°C. You can check this with a sugar thermometer or by drizzling a small amount into a cup of cold water. If the syrup is ready, it will form fine threads in the water. Remove the pan from the heat and add the additional citrus juice and the tequila, if using. Leave to cool down. The syrup should thicken as it cools.

Whisk the cream with the icing sugar until thick but not too stiff. Put the cream in the centre of the meringue and drizzle over some of the syrup. Give it a couple of quick stirs, then add a little more. Pile on the blueberries and drizzle over more syrup, leaving some to be added at the table.

OPEN-TOPPED MINCE PIES WITH FRANGIPANE

MAKES 24 | PREP: 30 MINS | COOK: 15-17 MINS

We're hoping these become your new Christmas classic, but they are great at any time of year. Going topless means there is half the amount of pastry so these pies are a bit lighter than usual and the frangipane makes for a lovely luxurious finish. They look so tempting too. Make your own mincemeat if you can, using our recipe on page 273. It's really easy.

Pastry
200g plain flour
50g ground almonds
50g icing sugar
125g butter, chilled and diced
1 egg yolk
1-2 tbsp iced water

Frangipane
85g butter, softened
85g caster sugar
2 eggs
100g ground almonds
15g plain flour
a few drops of almond
    extract (optional)
pinch of salt

To assemble
up to 400g mincemeat (see
    p.273 or shop-bought)
30g flaked almonds

First make the pastry. Put the flour, ground almonds, icing sugar and butter in a food processor and pulse until the mixture resembles fine breadcrumbs and is in danger of clumping together. Add the egg yolk and pulse again, then gradually add 1-2 tablespoons of the iced water, until the mixture comes together into a slightly tacky dough. Wrap well and chill.

Make the frangipane. Beat the butter and sugar together until very soft and aerated, then add the remaining ingredients with a pinch of salt. Mix to combine.

Preheat the oven to 200°C/Fan 180°C/Gas 6. Take the dough and roll it out to a thickness of about 3mm. Using a 7.5–8cm cutter, cut 24 rounds and use these to line 2 x 12-hole fairy cake tins.

Add a heaped teaspoon of mincemeat to each round of pastry, followed by a generously heaped teaspoon of the frangipane. Use a knife or spatula to spread the frangipane evenly over the mincemeat, adding a little more if necessary to seal round the edges, making sure the mincemeat is completely covered. Sprinkle with flaked almonds.

Bake the pies for 15-17 minutes, until the pastry is crisp and the frangipane is lightly browned and slightly domed. Leave to cool in the tins, then dust with icing sugar before serving. You can store the pies in an airtight tin for up to a week and they also freeze well.

CAKES & BAKES

CHERRY & CHOCOLATE CHEESECAKE

SERVES 8 | PREP: 30 MINS (PLUS CHILLING TIME) | COOK: 10 MINS

Cheesecake was one of the most popular desserts in our survey, so we felt we just had to come up with something special. We think you're going to love this one, which has a chocolate base and cherries in the filling. We like to use frozen cherries, as you can get them at any time of year, they keep their colour well and they're already pitted, so easier to deal with. Genius.

Chocolate base

200g biscuits, such as
   digestive or similar
75g dark or milk chocolate
75g butter

Cherry filling

300g frozen cherries,
   defrosted
2 tbsp icing sugar
2 tsp cornflour
1 tsp lemon juice
1 tsp Kirsch (optional)

Cream cheese filling

250g mascarpone cheese
350g cream cheese
100g icing sugar
1 tsp vanilla extract
pinch of salt
300ml double cream

Topping

fresh cherries, if in season,
   or chocolate curls

First make the base. Blitz the biscuits in a food processor or put them in a bag and give them a good bash with a rolling pin. Put the chocolate and butter in a heatproof bowl and place the bowl over a saucepan of simmering water. When they have melted, remove the bowl from the heat and add the biscuit crumbs. Stir to combine.

Line a 23cm cake tin with a circle of baking parchment. Press the crumbs into the base, making sure it comes up the sides a little, then put it in the fridge to chill until firm.

Put the cherries in a saucepan with their juices and add the sugar. Stir until the sugar has dissolved. Mix the cornflour with a little water and add this mixture to the cherries along with the lemon juice and Kirsch, if using. Stir until the sauce thickens a little. Leave to cool.

To make the cream cheese filling, beat the mascarpone, cream cheese, icing sugar and vanilla extract together with a pinch of salt until thick and smooth. Whisk the double cream in a separate bowl until thickened to the soft peak stage. Beat the cream into the cream cheese mixture until you have a stiff consistency that won't drop off a spoon.

Spoon the cherries into the centre of the cheesecake base, aiming to leave a border all the way round. Pile on the cream cheese filling, working from the edges inwards to make sure the cherries are sealed in. Smooth down as well as you can, then put the cake in the fridge to chill for several hours until completely set, preferably overnight.

If fresh cherries are in season, pile some on top or add some chocolate curls. You could even have some extra cream or ice cream on the side.

VICTORIA SPONGE

SERVES 8 | PREP: 30 MINS | COOK: 30-35 MINS

We hope the Women's Institute won't drum us out of the country for this one. It's inspired by a wonderful Italian olive oil sponge and it is tasty, zingy, soft and satisfying. A proper Pavarotti of a sponge. Don't use your best extra virgin oil though, as its flavour would be overwhelming. A light regular olive oil is best.

butter, for greasing
225g self-raising flour
2 tsp baking powder
pinch of salt
150ml olive oil
225g caster sugar
zest of 1 orange
½ tsp vanilla extract
4 eggs

Filling
250g double or whipping
    cream
1 tbsp icing sugar, plus
    extra for dusting
zest of ½ orange
3 tbsp raspberry jam
350g fresh raspberries,
    plus extra for decoration

Preheat the oven to 170°C/Fan 150°C/Gas 3½. Butter 2 x deep 20cm cake tins and line them with baking parchment.

Mix the flour and baking powder in a bowl or a stand mixer with a generous pinch of salt. Add the remaining cake ingredients and mix thoroughly – you should end up with a smooth, pourable batter. Divide this between the tins.

Bake in the preheated oven for 30–35 minutes until the cakes are well risen, golden-brown and firm but springy to the touch. Remove them from the oven and turn out on to a cooling rack. Leave to cool completely.

To make the filling, whisk the cream until thick and quite stiff, then stir in the icing sugar and orange zest. Spread the raspberry jam over the top of one of the cakes. Pile on two-thirds of the cream, then arrange the raspberries on top. Spread over the rest of the cream. Place the remaining cake on top and dust with icing sugar. Pile a few more raspberries on top.

This won't keep well, because of the fresh cream, so fill it just before you want to serve it and keep any leftovers in the fridge. Take the cake out of the fridge half an hour before you want to eat it.

CHOCOLATE CAKE

SERVES 8-10 | PREP: 30 MINS | COOK: 35-40 MINS

We just had to have a chocolate cake in this book, as it came up again and again in our survey, and this one is a knock-out. Simple enough to make every week but it can be dressed up with chocolate curls for a birthday or celebration. One thing to mention – be sure to use proper cocoa powder, not drinking chocolate.

100g dark chocolate
   (70% cocoa solids),
   broken up
25g cocoa
250ml just-boiled water
200g plain flour
2 tsp baking powder
½ tsp bicarbonate of soda
¼ tsp salt
200g butter, softened
250g light soft brown sugar
3 eggs
1 tsp vanilla extract
125ml soured cream

Buttercream icing
50g dark chocolate (70%
   cocoa solids), broken up
50g cocoa powder
2 tbsp just-boiled water
1 tsp vanilla extract
150g butter, softened
300g icing sugar
pinch of salt
1-2 tbsp milk

Decoration (optional)
chocolate curls

Preheat the oven to 180°C/Fan 160°C/Gas 4. Line 2 x 20cm sandwich tins with baking parchment.

Put the chocolate and cocoa in a bowl and pour over the hot water. Whisk until the chocolate has completely melted and you have a smooth liquid. Set aside.

Whisk the flour, baking powder, bicarbonate of soda and salt together.

Beat the butter and sugar together until very soft and aerated. Beat in the eggs, one at a time, then add all the remaining ingredients, including the chocolate liquid and the flour mixture, and combine, keeping mixing to a minimum. You should end up with a rich, pourable batter.

Divide the batter between the tins. Bake in the oven for 25–30 minutes until well risen and springy to the touch. Remove from the oven and leave the cakes in their tins for 10 minutes, before turning out on to a wire rack to cool.

To make the icing, put the chocolate, cocoa and water in a bowl and set over a pan of simmering water. Stir until the chocolate has completely melted, then add the vanilla extract. Remove the bowl from the heat and leave to cool slightly. Beat the butter until soft and aerated, then add the icing sugar and a pinch of salt. Continue to beat until smooth, then pour in the chocolate mixture. Continue to beat to combine and add up to 2 tablespoons of milk if the mixture is very stiff.

Spread a third of the icing over one of the cakes and place the other cake on top. Spread the rest of the icing over the top and sides of the cakes. Leave to set before serving. Add some lovely curls of chocolate, if you like.

CHAI CARROT CAKE

MAKES 12 PIECES | PREP: 30 MINS (PLUS INFUSING TIME | COOK: 40-45 MINS

Chai and chai-soaked raisins
1 tbsp loose tea or 1 teabag
5cm cinnamon stick, broken up
2 cloves
5 cardamom pods
½ tsp black peppercorns
1 mace blade
10g root ginger, sliced
150g raisins
2 tbsp caster sugar

Cake
175g melted butter or
    vegetable oil, plus extra
    for greasing
200g wholemeal self-raising
    flour
1 tsp baking powder
½ tsp bicarbonate of soda
½ tsp ground cinnamon
½ tsp ground cardamom
rasp of nutmeg
75g pistachios, finely chopped
pinch of salt
175g light soft brown sugar
3 eggs
200g carrots, grated

Cream cheese icing
100g icing sugar
100g butter, softened
zest of 1 lime
¼ tsp ground cardamom
¼ tsp ground cinnamon
200g cream cheese

To finish
25g pistachios, roughly chopped
2 tsp dried rose petals
    (optional)

This is carrot cake taken to another level. Soaking the raisins in the spicy chai tea adds so much flavour and if you don't want to gather all the spices you could use a chai teabag instead. Just brew the tea and use it to soak the raisins.

First infuse the raisins – ideally the day before making the cake. Tie the chai ingredients – tea, spices and ginger – into a piece of muslin and put them into a saucepan with 300ml of water. Bring to the boil, then simmer for 5 minutes. Add the raisins and sugar, simmer for a couple of minutes, then remove from the heat and leave to infuse as everything cools down. Leave to steep overnight if possible.

Preheat the oven to 200°C/Fan 180°C/Gas 6. Grease a 20cm square tin with a little butter or oil and line it with baking parchment. Mix the flour with the baking powder, bicarb, spices and pistachios and add a generous pinch of salt.

Pour the melted butter or oil into a separate large bowl and mix in the sugar. Beat in the eggs, then add the dry ingredients, followed by the carrots. Strain the raisins, reserving any remaining liquid, which should be quite syrupy. Stir the drained raisins into the cake – if the mixture seems too stiff, add enough of the reserved liquid to give a dropping consistency. Scrape the mixture into the tin, then bake in the oven for 35–40 minutes, until the cake is a rich brown and springy but firm to the touch. Leave to cool in the tin for 10 minutes, then turn the cake out on to a cooling rack.

To make the icing, sift the icing sugar into a bowl and beat in the butter, lime zest and spices. Continue to beat until the mixture is light and aerated, then beat in the cream cheese until smooth. Cover and chill in the fridge until firm.

Spread the icing over the cake and sprinkle over the pistachios and rose petals, if using. Cut into squares to serve.

BANANA BREAD WITH PEANUT BUTTER SWIRL

MAKES 1 LOAF | PREP: 20 MINS | COOK: 50-60 MINS

We heard that banana bread was everyone's lockdown favourite bake and we've taken it up a notch. With our addition of a peanut butter, cream cheese, chocolate and maple syrup swirl it's become a superstar. One for the peanut butter lovers out there.

175g plain flour
2 tsp baking powder
1 tsp cinnamon
pinch of salt
125g butter, melted
150g light soft brown sugar
2 eggs
3 large ripe bananas, mashed

Peanut butter swirl
125g peanut butter
    (preferably crunchy)
75g cream cheese
50ml maple syrup
50g chocolate chips
    (dark or milk)

Preheat the oven to 180°C/Fan 160°C/Gas 4. Line a large (900g) loaf tin with baking parchment.

Mix the flour with the baking powder, cinnamon and a large pinch of salt. Put the butter into a large bowl and whisk in the sugar. Beat in the eggs, then add the flour mixture, making sure everything is thoroughly combined. Stir in the bananas.

Mix all the ingredients for the swirl in a separate bowl.

Put half the banana bread batter in the loaf tin. Spread over the peanut butter mixture and top with the remaining banana bread batter. Take a spoon and stir them together very briefly, not to combine, but to spread the swirl through the batter – 2 or 3 turns at the most.

Bake in the preheated oven for 50–60 minutes until the banana bread has slightly shrunk away from the sides and is springy to the touch. Leave to cool in the tin for 10 minutes, then turn out on to a cooling rack. This can be kept in an airtight tin for up to a week.

BARA BRITH

MAKES 1 LOAF | PREP: 15 MINS (PLUS SOAKING TIME) | COOK: 1-1¼ HOURS

Bara brith is a traditional Welsh tea loaf and for this one the fruit is steeped in rooibos tea and lemon zest overnight for extra flavour. This is moist and delicious, with or without butter, and there's nothing better with a cuppa for an afternoon pick-you-up.

400g mixed dried fruit
   (sultanas, raisins and
   currants)
25g candied peel, finely
   chopped (optional)
350ml strong tea, made
   with rooibos tea bags
zest of 1 lemon
100g light soft brown sugar
2 eggs, beaten
300g self-raising flour
   (white or wholemeal)
1 tsp cinnamon
rasp of nutmeg
pinch of salt

Put the dried fruit and the candied peel, if using, into a large bowl and cover with the stewed tea and lemon zest. You can leave the teabags in to intensify the flavour. Cover and leave to stand overnight.

The next day, preheat the oven to 160°C/Fan 140°C/Gas 3 and line a large loaf tin with baking parchment.

Stir the sugar into the fruit, followed by the eggs. Mix the flour with the spices and a large pinch of salt and add this to the fruit mixture, stirring until well combined with no streaks of flour.

Scrape the mixture into the prepared tin and bake for an 1-1¼ hours, checking after an hour – it's done when it is springy to the touch and has slightly shrunk away from the sides of the tin.

Leave the cake to cool in the tin, then wrap it in baking parchment. Store in an airtight tin for a day or so before eating if possible – the flavours will develop and the crust will become sticky.

Serve on its own or thickly spread with butter.

DOUBLE-DECKER BROWNIES

MAKES 12 PIECES | PREP: 25 MINS | COOK: ABOUT 35 MINS

This is proper OTT – tiffin bar meets rocky road to make one of the most seriously luxurious brownies you will ever taste. Eat two if you dare! We used chocolate Viennese sandwich biscuits for the base, but bourbons would also work well.

150g butter
225g granulated sugar
75g cocoa powder
100g raisins
75g rum
75g plain flour
½ tsp baking powder
pinch of salt
2 eggs
1 tsp vanilla extract
50g milk chocolate chips

Extras
150g chocolate biscuits,
    broken up
150g soft nougat, chopped
    into chunks
50g milk chocolate

Line a square brownie tin with baking parchment. Put the butter, sugar and cocoa into a heatproof bowl and place over a pan of simmering water. Leave to melt, then stir to combine – the mixture will probably be a little grainy, but should also be quite runny. Leave to cool slightly. Preheat the oven to 160°C/Fan 140°C/Gas 3.

Put the raisins and rum in a small saucepan and bring to the boil. Simmer until most of the rum has been absorbed or boiled away, then leave to cool. Mix the flour with the baking powder and salt.

Beat the eggs into the butter and sugar mixture, followed by the vanilla and the flour mix. Drain the raisins and stir them in, along with the chocolate chips.

Arrange the chocolate biscuits over the base of the tin. Carefully scrape the brownie mix over them, covering the biscuits completely, then smooth the top over with a spatula. Push the pieces of nougat into the brownie batter.

Bake in the oven for 20–25 minutes until the top is crisp and shiny and a skewer comes out with a few crumbs clinging to it. Leave to cool completely in the tin and if possible, leave in the fridge overnight – the texture will be much better.

Melt the chocolate in a bowl over a pan of simmering water, then drizzle it over the brownies. Cut into 12 pieces. The brownies keep well in an airtight tin for up to a week – if you let them!

COFFEE, WALNUT & DATE COOKIES

MAKES ABOUT 24 | PREP: 15 MINS (PLUS CHILLING TIME) | COOK: 9-11 MINS

Here are all the things we love in a cake translated to cookie form – a proper tea-time delight. A word of advice – don't chop the nuts or dates too small, as they'll interfere with the texture of the cookie; they work better in quite big chunks.

150g plain flour
½ tsp bicarbonate of soda
2 tbsp espresso powder
    (ground if in granules)
½ tsp salt
110g butter, softened
100g granulated sugar
75g soft light brown sugar
1 tsp vanilla extract
1 egg
50g walnuts, roughly
    chopped
50g dates, roughly chopped

Whisk the flour, bicarbonate of soda and coffee powder together in a bowl with the salt. Set aside.

Beat the butter with the sugars until very soft. Beat in the vanilla extract and the egg, then add the flour mixture, walnuts and dates all at once. Fold them in, keeping mixing to an absolute minimum. Cover and chill in the fridge for at least an hour, but preferably overnight.

When you are ready to bake the cookies, preheat the oven to 180°C/Fan 160°C/Gas 4 and line 2 baking trays with non-stick baking parchment. Drop heaped tablespoons of the mixture on to the prepared baking trays – try to avoid smoothing them down as you do so and make sure they are well spaced out as they will spread. You should get about 24 cookies.

Bake in the oven for 9–11 minutes, until well spread out and very lightly golden around the edges. They will seem very soft but don't worry – they will firm up ` as they cool. Leave on the baking tray for 5 minutes, then transfer to a cooling rack to finish cooling. Store in an airtight tin.

MANCHESTER TART FLAPJACK

MAKES 9 PIECES | PREP: 25 MINS (PLUS CHILLING TIME) | COOK: ABOUT 30 MINS

Manchester tart was a school dinner favourite for us and we've teamed it up with a flapjack to make what we hope will be a new classic. The flapjack base has a bit of flour and egg added to give it a slightly firmer texture. Then the topping has all the delights of a classic Manchester tart – custard, raspberry jam and coconut. And don't forget the cherries. Epic!

Base
75g butter
50g light brown soft sugar
1 tbsp (25g) golden syrup
pinch of salt
175g porridge oats
50g flour
1 egg

Custard
500ml milk
250ml double or whipping
   cream
vanilla pod, split
5 egg yolks
100g caster sugar
50g cornflour or custard
   powder

To assemble
5 tbsp raspberry jam
fresh raspberries (optional)
35g desiccated coconut
maraschino cherries

Line a square brownie tin (preferably loose-based) with baking parchment or a non-stick liner. Preheat the oven to 170°C/Fan 150°C/Gas 3½.

Melt the butter, sugar and golden syrup in a saucepan with a pinch of salt. Remove from the heat and beat in the oats, followed by the flour and the egg.

Spread the mixture over the base of the tin. It is quite sticky so it can be tricky to work with. Our tip is to run your hands under cold water and use them to pat the mixture into place, making it as smooth and as even as you can. Bake in the oven for about 15 minutes until the mixture has set and is browning round the edges. Remove from the oven and leave to cool.

To make the custard, heat the milk and cream together with the vanilla pod until just below boiling point. Remove from the heat and leave to cool a little. Beat the egg yolks and sugar together in a bowl until thick and creamy, then beat in the cornflour or custard powder. Pour the milk and cream mixture from a height on to the eggs, whisking as you do so, then tip everything back into the saucepan.

Stir the custard on a medium-low heat, until you notice it starting to thicken at the bottom. Whisk constantly at this point so the custard stays smooth and lump free. It will be ready when it is starting to bubble, has thickened considerably but is still pourable. Remove from the heat and leave to cool to room temperature, whisking regularly to prevent a skin from forming. Take out the vanilla pod.

To assemble, spread the jam over the base. Dot over fresh raspberries, if using, then spread the custard over the top, smoothing it with a palette knife. Sprinkle with the coconut and decorate with one or several maraschino cherries. Chill for several hours until completely set.

Remove from the tin, then cut into squares to serve.

CARAWAY & LEMON SHORTBREAD

MAKES 20-24 PIECES | PREP: 15 MINS (PLUS CHILLING TIME) | COOK: 20-60 MINS

There's nothing like a piece of good old-fashioned shortbread, but we think flavouring it with subtle hints of caraway and lemon brings a nice 21st-century twist to this much-loved classic.

250g plain flour

75g ground rice or fine
    semolina

pinch of salt

200g butter, softened

100g caster sugar, plus
    2 tbsp for sprinkling

1½ tsp caraway seeds,
    lightly crushed

zest of 1 lemon

Line a 20 x 20cm square baking tin with baking parchment.

Put the flour and ground rice or semolina in a bowl or the bowl of a stand mixer. Add a generous pinch of salt. Add the butter, sugar, caraway seeds and lemon zest. Using electric beaters or the beater attachment, mix until the ingredients come together into a solid mass. Alternatively, rub the butter into the dry ingredients until the mixture starts to clump together, then knead it into a ball. Press the mixture evenly into the prepared tin. Chill in the fridge for at least half an hour.

Preheat the oven to 150°C/Fan 130°C/Gas 2. Sprinkle the shortbread with the 2 tablespoons of caster sugar and make indentations over the top with a fork – most of these will disappear but they help the shortbread bake evenly.

Bake in the oven for about an hour until the shortbread is lightly browned. Remove from the oven and cut into fingers or whatever shape you like.

For a quicker bake, but longer prep, roll or pat out the dough into a square and cut into pieces. Arrange them on a large baking tray. Chill as above and bake for about 20 minutes.

CHEESE & ANCHOVY BISCUITS

MAKES 24 | PREP: 15 MINS (PLUS CHILLING TIME) | COOK: 10 MINS

We've gone crackers for these little beauties – something for those of you with a savoury tooth. They're great with cheese or they're tasty enough to serve on their own with drinks. If you like, you can freeze half the dough and save it for another time.

125g plain flour
125g butter, chilled and diced
1 x 30g can of anchovies (drained weight), finely chopped
125g Parmesan cheese, grated
1 tbsp finely chopped rosemary (optional)
2 tsp chilli flakes (optional)
black pepper

Rub the flour into the butter until the mixture resembles coarse breadcrumbs. Add some black pepper (no salt, as the anchovies provide all the salt you need), the anchovies and Parmesan. Mix together until you have a smooth dough.

Divide the mixture into 2 even pieces and roll each into a log of about 12cm long. Wrap well and chill for at least an hour until very firm.

When you are ready to bake the biscuits, preheat the oven to 170°C/Fan 150°C/Gas 3½. Cut each of the logs into 12 rounds (the easiest way to do this evenly is to cut it in half, then quarters, then each quarter into 3). Line 2 baking trays with baking parchment.

Arrange the biscuits on the trays and sprinkle with the rosemary or chilli flakes or both. Bake in the oven for about 10 minutes – the biscuits should be lightly coloured but not brown.

Cool for a few minutes on a rack, but best eaten slightly warm.

CHEESE & RED ONION SCONES

MAKES 12 | PREP: 20 MINS | COOK: 12-15 MINS

Scones are one of the nation's favourite teatime treats. We love a good cheese scone and these little beauties are dialled up to 11. The onion topping is just the job to finish off our creation. Don't be shy with the butter when you're enjoying these.

450g self-raising flour, plus extra for dusting

1½ tsp baking powder

1 tsp sugar

1 tsp salt

125g butter, chilled and diced

100g Gruyère cheese, grated

50g Parmesan cheese, grated

1 tbsp za'atar or 1 tsp dried thyme

150ml milk

1 egg

1 egg, beaten with 1 tbsp water

Onion topping

1 tbsp olive oil

15g butter

2 red onions, sliced

a few thyme leaves

1 tbsp caster sugar

1 tbsp red wine or sherry vinegar

sea and black pepper

First make the onion topping. Heat the olive oil and butter in a lidded sauté pan and when the butter has melted, add the onions and thyme. Cook over a gentle heat, partially covered but stirring regularly, until the onions are soft, translucent and collapsed. Add the sugar and vinegar and season well with salt and pepper. Turn up the heat and cook, stirring regularly, until the onions are caramelised and slightly jammy.

Preheat the oven to 200°C/Fan 180°C/Gas 6 and line a baking tray with baking parchment. Put the flour, baking powder and sugar into a food processor or stand mixer and add the salt and butter. Mix until the texture resembles fine breadcrumbs. Stir in 65g of the Gruyère, then the Parmesan and za'atar or thyme. Mix the milk and egg together, then add this to the mixture. Keep mixing to an absolute minimum, then turn out the dough on to a lightly floured surface.

Knead very gently and briefly to make sure the dough has come together, then pat out into a round about 3cm thick. Dip a 6cm cutter in flour to make cutting out easier. Cut out rounds – avoid twisting as you do so – and place them on the baking tray. Squeeze together the offcuts and cut again – you should end up with 12 tall scones. Brush with beaten egg, then spread the onions over the top, pressing them down very lightly. Sprinkle with the remaining Gruyère.

Bake in the preheated oven for 12–15 minutes until well risen and craggy. Serve warm straight from the oven or leave to cool. Store in an airtight container.

BASICS
& SIDES

VEGETABLE STOCK

MAKES ABOUT 1.5 LITRES

1 tsp olive oil

2 large onions, roughly
chopped

3 large carrots, chopped

200g squash or pumpkin,
unpeeled, diced

4 celery sticks, sliced

2 leeks, sliced

100ml white wine or
vermouth

large thyme sprig

large parsley sprig

1 bay leaf

a few peppercorns

Heat the olive oil in a large saucepan. Add all the vegetables and fry them over a high heat, stirring regularly, until they start to brown and caramelise around the edges. This will take at least 10 minutes. Add the white wine or vermouth and boil until it has evaporated away.

Cover the vegetables with 2 litres of water and add the herbs and peppercorns. Bring to the boil, then turn the heat down to a gentle simmer. Cook the stock, uncovered, for about an hour, stirring every so often.

Check the stock – the colour should have some depth to it. Strain it through a colander or a sieve lined with muslin or kitchen paper into a bowl. Store it in the fridge for up to a week or freeze it.

FISH STOCK

MAKES ABOUT 1.5 LITRES

1.5kg fish heads and bones
from white fish (ask your
fishmonger)

1 tbsp salt

2 tbsp olive oil

1 onion, finely chopped

2 leeks, finely sliced

½ fennel bulb, finely chopped

1 celery stick, sliced

2 garlic cloves, sliced

200ml white wine

bouquet garni made up of
2 sprigs each of parsley,
tarragon and thyme)

2 bay leaves

a few peppercorns

1 piece of thinly pared
lemon zest

Put the fish heads and bones in a bowl, cover them with cold water and add the salt. Leave to stand for an hour, then drain and wash thoroughly under running water. This process helps to draw out any blood from the fish and gives you a much clearer, fresher-tasting stock.

Heat the olive oil in a large saucepan. Add the onion, leeks, fennel, celery and garlic. Cook the vegetables over a medium heat for several minutes until they start to soften without taking on any colour.

Add the fish heads and bones and pour over the wine. Bring to the boil, then add 2 litres of water. Bring back to the boil, skim off any mushroom-coloured foam that appears on the surface, then turn the heat down to a very slow simmer. Add the herbs, peppercorns and lemon zest and leave to simmer for 30 minutes, skimming off any foam every so often.

Strain the stock through a colander or sieve into a bowl, then line the sieve with muslin or kitchen paper and strain the stock again. Don't push it through as that will result in a cloudier stock. Leave to cool, then keep in the fridge for 3–4 days or freeze it.

CHICKEN STOCK

MAKES ABOUT 1 LITRE

at least 1 chicken carcass,
    pulled apart
4 chicken wings (optional)
1 onion, unpeeled, cut into
    quarters
1 large carrot, cut into
    large chunks
2 celery sticks, roughly
    chopped
1 leek, roughly chopped
1 tsp black peppercorns
3 bay leaves
large parsley sprig
small thyme sprig
a few garlic cloves,
    unpeeled (optional)

Put the chicken bones and the wings, if using, into a saucepan, just large enough for all the chicken to fit quite snugly. Cover with cold water, bring to the boil, then skim off any foam that collects. Add the remaining ingredients and turn the heat down to a very low simmer. Partially cover the pan with a lid.

Leave the stock to simmer for about 3 hours, then remove the pan from the heat. Strain the stock through a colander or a sieve lined with muslin or kitchen paper into a bowl.

The stock can be used right away, although it is best to skim off most of the fat that will collect on the top. If you don't need the stock immediately, leave it to cool. The fat will set on top and will be much easier to remove.

You can keep the stock in the fridge for up to 5 days, or freeze it. If you want to make a larger amount of stock, save up your chicken carcasses in the freezer or add more chicken wings.

BEEF STOCK

MAKES ABOUT 2 LITRES

1.5.kg beef bones, including
    marrow bones if possible,
    cut into small lengths
500g piece of beef shin or
    any cheap, fairly lean cut
2 onions, unpeeled, roughly
    chopped
1 leek, roughly chopped
2 celery sticks, roughly
    chopped
2 carrots, roughly chopped
2 tomatoes
½ tsp peppercorns
bouquet garni made up of
    large sprigs of thyme,
    parsley and 2 bay leaves

Put the beef bones and meat into a large saucepan and cover them with cold water – at least 3-3.5 litres. Bring the water to the boil and when a starchy, mushroom-grey foam appears, start skimming. Keep on skimming as the foam turns white and continue until it has almost stopped developing.

Add the vegetables, peppercorns and bouquet garni, turn down the heat until the stock is simmering very gently, then partially cover the pan with a lid. Leave to simmer for 3-4 hours.

Line a sieve or colander with 2 layers of muslin or a tea towel and place it over a large bowl. Ladle the stock into the sieve or colander to strain it. Remove the meat and set it aside, then discard everything else. Pour the strained stock into a large container and leave it to cool. The fat should solidify on top of the stock and will be very easy to remove. You can keep the stock in the fridge for 2 or 3 days or freeze it.

Don't chuck out the piece of meat – it's good in sandwiches or can be sliced, fried and added to salads.

ONION GRAVY

SERVES 4

50g butter

3 onions, finely sliced

1 tsp sugar

100ml red wine

large thyme sprig

1 bay leaf

600ml well-flavoured beef
   stock or consommé

dash of Worcestershire
   sauce (optional)

sea salt and black pepper

To thicken (optional)

1 tbsp flour

15g butter, softened

Melt the butter in a wide saucepan or a lidded sauté pan and add the onions. Sauté gently until they are soft and translucent, then stir in the sugar and turn up the heat. Continue to cook, stirring regularly, until the onions are a rich brown and caramelised.

Pour in the red wine, add the herbs and bring to the boil. Allow the wine to reduce down by at least two-thirds, then pour in the stock or consommé. Add the Worcestershire sauce, if using, and season with salt and pepper. Bring to the boil, then turn down the heat, cover and leave to simmer for 10 minutes.

The gravy can be served like this, but you can thicken it, if you prefer. To do this, mash the flour and butter together, then whisk a teaspoon at a time into the simmering gravy. Keep whisking until the mixture is dissolved and the gravy is the consistency you like.

CHICKEN VELOUTÉ GRAVY

SERVES 4

25g butter

1 shallot, very finely chopped

1 bay leaf

thyme or tarragon sprig

25g plain flour

100ml white wine

600ml well-flavoured
   chicken stock

100ml double cream
   (optional)

sea salt and black pepper

Melt the butter in a saucepan and add the shallot, bay leaf and either thyme or tarragon. Sauté until the shallot is very soft and translucent, then stir in the flour. Stir until you have a lightly toasted paste or roux – cook it for long enough for the flour to lose its raw aroma.

Turn up the heat and pour in the wine. It should bubble up immediately. Stir vigorously – the roux should thicken and pull away from the base of the pan. Make sure it is smooth, then start adding the chicken stock, gradually to start with. Allow each addition to bubble up, then stir until smooth. Continue until you have added all the stock. The sauce should have the consistency of thin custard.

Season with salt and black pepper and simmer gently for 5 minutes. For a richer sauce, add the cream and simmer gently for another couple of minutes. Remove the herbs just before serving and strain the gravy if you don't want the texture of the shallots.

VINDALOO SPICE PASTE

MAKES 1 SMALL JAR

8 green cardamom pods

1 tsp black peppercorns

8 cloves

5cm piece of cinnamon stick

1 tsp cumin seeds

½ tsp coriander seeds

2 tbsp Kashmiri chilli powder

1 tsp turmeric

1 tbsp tamarind purée

1 tbsp vinegar (cider or
   red wine)

25g root ginger, roughly
   grated

4 garlic cloves, roughly
   chopped

Put the whole spices in a dry frying pan – preferably not a non-stick one. Toast until they have a strong aroma, then remove and cool.

Remove the shells from the cardamom pods, then blitz all the whole spices in a grinder. Transfer to a food processor with the remaining ingredients and blitz to a paste, adding water to help it combine if necessary. Spoon into a jar or bowl and keep it in the fridge.

MEDIUM CURRY POWDER

MAKES 1 SMALL JAR

1 tbsp cumin seeds

1 tbsp coriander seeds

1 tsp mustard seeds

1 tsp nigella seeds

½ tsp fenugreek seeds

3cm piece of cinnamon stick,
   broken up

6 dried curry leaves
   (optional)

1 tsp ground turmeric

1 tsp chilli powder

1 tsp sweet paprika

1 tsp garlic granules

¼ tsp asafoetida

Put all the whole spices and the curry leaves, if using, into a dry frying pan – preferably not a non-stick one. Toast over a medium heat until the aroma is strong and the mustard seeds are popping.

Transfer the toasted spices and curry leaves to a bowl to cool, then grind them to a fine powder in a spice grinder or with a pestle and mortar. Mix with the turmeric, chilli powder, sweet paprika, garlic granules and asafoetida and store in an airtight jar.

CARIBBEAN CURRY POWDER

MAKES 1 SMALL JAR

4cm piece of cinnamon stick, broken up

2 tbsp coriander seeds

2 tsp cumin seeds

1 tsp mustard seeds

1 tsp white peppercorns

½ tsp allspice berries

½ tsp fenugreek

seeds from 6 cardamom pods

4 cloves

2 mace blades

2 dried bay leaves

1 tbsp ground turmeric

½ tsp onion salt

Put all the whole spices and the bay leaves in a dry frying pan – preferably not a non-stick one. Toast the spices over a medium heat, shaking regularly, until the aroma intensifies and the mustard seeds are popping. Transfer to a bowl to cool.

Grind the spices in a spice grinder or with a pestle and mortar to form a fine powder, then mix with the turmeric and onion salt. Store in an airtight jar.

TACO SEASONING

MAKES 1 SMALL JAR

1 tbsp garlic powder

1 tbsp onion powder

1 tbsp dried oregano

1 tbsp sweet paprika

1 tbsp ground cumin

1 tbsp ground coriander

1 tbsp chilli powder or flakes

1 tsp cinnamon

1 tsp sugar

1 tsp salt

Mix everything together and transfer to a clean, dry jar. Use mild or hot chilli powder depending on the level of heat you like.

MIDDLE EASTERN (BAHARAT) SPICE MIX

MAKES 1 SMALL JAR

1 tbsp black pepper
1 tbsp smoked paprika
1 tbsp ground coriander
1 tbsp ground cumin
1 tsp ground cinnamon
1 tsp ground allspice
1 tsp ground cardamom
½ tsp ground cloves
rasp of nutmeg

Mix everything together and store in a clean, dry jar.

CAJUN SPICE MIX

MAKES 1 SMALL JAR

1 tbsp salt
1 tbsp smoked paprika
1 tbsp garlic powder
1 tbsp onion powder
2 tsp dried oregano
1 tsp dried thyme
1 tsp ground black pepper
1 tsp cayenne

Mix everything together and store in a clean, dry jar.

BROWN OR WILD RICE

SERVES 4

250g brown or wild rice
500ml water or stock
1 tsp salt

Brown rice can be cooked faster by fiercely boiling in more water, but the following method gives much more control and the best texture.

Put the rice in a saucepan – there is no need to rinse it first. Cover with the water or stock and add the salt. Bring to the boil, then turn down the heat to a relatively fast simmer and cover. Leave to cook for 30–35 minutes, until most of the water has been absorbed and the rice is tender.

Remove the pan from the heat, then place a folded tea towel between the pan and the lid. Leave the rice to steam in its own heat for another 10 minutes for perfectly fluffy, tender rice.

BASMATI OR LONG-GRAIN RICE

SERVES 4

200g basmati or long-grain
    rice
generous pinch of salt

Rinse the rice thoroughly until the water runs clear, then put it in a bowl and cover with cold water. Leave to stand for 30 minutes, then drain thoroughly and transfer to a pan.

Add the salt and cover with 300ml of water. Bring to the boil, then turn down the heat and leave the rice to cook for 10 minutes. At this point, most of the water should have been absorbed and the rice should have turned from a greyish, semi-translucence to an opaque white. Take the pan off the heat.

Fold a tea towel and put it over the pan, then put the lid back on top. Leave the rice to steam for a further 5 minutes – the tea towel will help the rice become fluffy by absorbing excess moisture. Fluff up the rice with a fork and serve.

Soaking the rice does give the best results but if you don't have time, rinse it well and cook for 15 minutes instead of 10.

SAUERKRAUT

MAKES 2 LARGE JARS

1 white or green cabbage
    (about 1kg)
1 tbsp sea salt
1 tsp caraway or dill seeds
    (optional)
1 tsp celery seeds
spring or filtered water,
    if needed

It's important to have large, wide-rimmed jars for this because there needs to be enough room at the top for the weights and for gas to build up. Sterilise the jars in a hot dishwasher cycle or wash them in hot, soapy water, rinse thoroughly and dry them out in a low oven. Make sure the jars are completely dry before filling.

Slice the cabbage into wedges and cut out the core. Shred the wedges as finely as you can and slice the core into thin strips, then into matchsticks. Put all this in a large bowl and add the sea salt. Rub the salt into the cabbage until the cabbage starts to give out liquid – droplets will start to appear on the surface – and you can feel the texture start to change. Keep massaging until the cabbage looks wet and is sitting in a pool of water. If it is resistant, you can weigh it down and leave it to stand for an hour, but this shouldn't be necessary.

Stir in any seeds you like, then pack the cabbage into the jars, pressing down as much as possible to make sure there are no air pockets. Reserve the brining liquid. There should be enough room at the top of the jar to weigh the cabbage down, so don't fill it more than three-quarters of the way up.

Divide the brining liquid between the jars. If it doesn't quite cover the cabbage you can add a small amount of filtered or spring water – not tap water, which is chlorinated and can inhibit the fermentation process. Then weigh down the cabbage. Use special glass weights for this or fill a plastic bag with water, or if there is room, use a shallow ramekin. Make sure that all the cabbage is sitting below the surface of the liquid – it is important that it doesn't come into contact with the air. Seal the jars.

Leave the jars somewhere cool and dark for several days, checking every day and loosening the lids to make sure the build-up of gases within the jars is released. You should start seeing small air bubbles appear after a couple of days.

Taste the sauerkraut after 4–5 days. If you are happy with what should be a pleasantly sour flavour, remove the weights and transfer the jars to the fridge. It will keep fermenting at a much slower rate, so do keep checking the lid to make sure the gases aren't building up. You can start eating it immediately or leave for as long as you like – up to several months. Once opened, eat within a few weeks.

KIMCHI

MAKES ENOUGH FOR A 1-LITRE JAR

1 Chinese cabbage or Savoy
    cabbage

1 large carrot, cut into
    matchsticks

bunch of spring onions,
    roughly chopped (include
    the green parts)

20g sea salt

spring or filtered water,
    if needed

Paste

1 tbsp chilli powder – Korean
    if possible, if not Kashmiri

1 tbsp sweet paprika

1 tsp sugar

15g root ginger, grated

4 garlic cloves, crushed

2 tbsp fish sauce or
    soy sauce

1 tsp shrimp paste (optional)

First prepare a large 1-litre jar. Sterilise the jar either in a hot dishwasher cycle or wash it in hot, soapy water, rinse it thoroughly and dry out in a low oven. Make sure the jar is completely dry before filling.

Next, brine the vegetables. Trim the base of the Chinese cabbage and cut it into 6 pieces, lengthwise. Then cut each piece into 2cm strips. Put these in a bowl along with the carrot and spring onions. Sprinkle over the salt and rub it into the vegetables until they start to release liquid – it will start with a few droplets of water appearing on the surface. Cover with a plate and weigh the plate down with a couple of tins.

Leave to stand for at least 2 hours, then drain – quite a bit of liquid will have come out of the vegetables. Rinse the vegetables, using spring or filtered water (tap water contains chlorine which can inhibit the fermentation process), and taste for saltiness. If it's still too salty, rinse one more time. Drain thoroughly.

Mix all the paste ingredients together and pour this over the vegetables. Stir to combine, then pack them into the prepared jar, pushing everything down to make sure you don't leave any air pockets. Seal and leave somewhere cool and dark for 24 hours. Remove the lid and press everything down again, then reseal and leave for another 24 hours. You should start to see small bubbles appear on the surface and it should smell pleasantly sour. You can transfer the kimchi to the fridge at this point, or you can keep fermenting it at room temperature, tasting daily until it has the flavour you like. Keep this going for up to 2 weeks.

Once the kimchi is in the fridge it will keep fermenting and improving in flavour, but the process will slow down considerably. It will keep in the fridge indefinitely.

GUACAMOLE

SERVES 4

juice of 1 lime
2 or 3 ripe avocadoes
sea salt and black pepper

Optional extras
½ red onion, finely chopped
1 medium tomato,
    finely diced
2 jalapeño chillies,
    finely chopped
handful of coriander,
    finely chopped

Before you start preparing the avocados, put half the lime juice in a bowl with a teaspoon of salt. Cut the avocadoes in half, remove the stones and peel, then roughly chop the flesh. Put the flesh in the bowl of lime juice and mash very lightly – the end result should be fairly chunky.

Add the remaining lime juice and check for seasoning. We like to keep this simple with just avocado and lime juice to serve with dishes like fajitas which have a lot going on. Alternatively, add some of the optional extras and serve as a dip.

TOMATO SALSA

SERVES 4

1 small red onion,
    finely diced
juice and zest of ½ lime
250g ripe tomatoes,
    finely chopped
½ red pepper, very finely
    chopped
1 hot red chilli, very finely
    chopped (optional)
2 tbsp olive oil
1 tsp sherry vinegar
pinch of cinnamon
pinch of sugar
small bunch of coriander,
    finely chopped
sea salt and black pepper

Mix the red onion with the lime juice and sprinkle with half a teaspoon of salt. Leave to stand for half an hour.

Mix the red onion, undrained, with the tomatoes and the remaining ingredients. Season with black pepper (there is already plenty of salt on the onion) and taste. Adjust the salt, vinegar and sugar as necessary and leave to stand for half an hour before serving.

WHITE BEAN SALAD

SERVES 4

200g dried cannellini beans
bouquet garni made up of
   1 bay leaf, 1 thyme sprig
   2 parsley sprigs, 1 tsp
   lightly crushed black
   peppercorns, 1 slice
   of onion
3 tbsp olive oil
1 red onion, finely sliced
1 garlic clove, finely chopped
small bunch of parsley,
   finely chopped
zest of ½ lemon
1 tbsp lemon juice
1 tsp sherry vinegar
sea salt and black pepper

First soak the beans. The best method is to put them in a bowl, cover them with water and leave overnight, then drain. Alternatively, if you forget to do this, try a quick soak. Put the beans in a saucepan and cover them with water. Add a teaspoon of salt and bring the water to the boil, then immediately remove the pan from the heat and leave the beans to stand for an hour. Drain.

Whichever soaking method you've used, put the beans in a large saucepan and cover them with fresh water. Add a teaspoon of salt and the bouquet garni, then bring to the boil and skim off any mushroom-coloured foam. Boil for 10 minutes, then turn the heat down to a simmer and cook until the beans are tender. How long this takes will vary, depending on your beans, but it usually takes at least an hour and up to an hour and a half.

Drain the beans - reserve the cooking liquid and use it to make soup, if you like. Discard the bouquet garni.

Heat the olive oil in a frying pan and lightly sauté the red onion until softened but still with a bit of bite. Add the garlic and cook for a further minute. Remove the pan from the heat and add the beans. Stir in the remaining ingredients and taste for seasoning, adding more salt and some black pepper.

If you prefer, you can make this with canned beans. Just drain the beans and add them to the onion mixture.

ROAST NEW POTATOES WITH GARLIC & ROSEMARY

SERVES 4

1kg new potatoes, unpeeled
50ml olive oil
1 garlic bulb
a few rosemary sprigs
sea salt and black pepper

Preheat the oven to 200°C/Fan 180°C/Gas 6.

Cut any larger potatoes into chunks, then put them in a saucepan and cover them with water. Add salt, then bring to the boil and simmer for 5 minutes. Drain well.

Pour the olive oil into a roasting tin and heat for a couple of minutes in the oven. Remove and add the potatoes, carefully shaking them around to coat them in the hot oil.

Separate the garlic bulb into cloves but leave them unpeeled. Add these to the tin, along with all but one of the sprigs of rosemary. Season with plenty of sea salt and black pepper.

Put the roasting tin in the oven and roast the potatoes for about 45 minutes, turning them over every so often. Chop the spikes from the reserved sprig of rosemary and toss them over the potatoes.

DAL

SERVES 4

1 tbsp coconut oil
1 onion, finely sliced
12 curry leaves
1 tsp cumin seeds
1 tsp mustard seeds
15g root ginger, grated
4 garlic cloves, crushed
　　or grated
2 tbsp finely chopped
　　coriander stems
½ tsp turmeric
pinch of asafoetida
200g red lentils, well rinsed
200g canned tomatoes,
　　puréed
salt and black pepper

To serve
coriander leaves
a few green chillies, sliced

Heat the coconut oil in a large saucepan and add the onion. Sauté over a medium-high heat until it starts to colour, then add the curry leaves, cumin seeds and mustard seeds. When the seeds start to pop, stir in the ginger, garlic, coriander stems and spices. Stir for a couple of minutes, then add the lentils and tomatoes. Add a litre of water and season with salt and pepper.

Bring to the boil, then turn down the heat and simmer for about 20 minutes until the lentils have swelled and thickened. Serve garnished with coriander leaves and green chillies.

MINCEMEAT

MAKES ABOUT 3 X 450G JARS

200g raisins

200g sultanas

100g dried prunes, finely chopped

100g dried sour cherries, finely chopped (or dried blueberries or cranberries)

100g candied peel (preferably orange), finely chopped

zest and juice of 2 oranges

100ml sherry (medium sweet, such as amontillado)

75ml brandy or Kirsch

1 Bramley apple, peeled, cored and finely diced

1 tsp ground cinnamon

½ tsp ground cardamom

½ tsp ground allspice

a good rasp of nutmeg

1 tbsp orange blossom water (optional)

250g light soft brown sugar

100g suet

First prepare the jars. Sterilise them either in a hot dishwasher cycle or wash them in hot, soapy water, rinse thoroughly and dry out in a low oven. Make sure the jars are completely dry before filling.

Put all the dried fruit – the raisins, sultanas, prunes, cherries and peel – into a large saucepan with the orange zest and juice and add the sherry and brandy. Bring to the boil, then remove the pan from the heat. Stir thoroughly and leave to stand for an hour.

Add all the remaining ingredients and heat again, this time very gently, until the suet has melted. Spoon into the sterilised jars, then leave to cool before covering. Store somewhere cool and dark and leave for at least 2 weeks but preferably a month before using.

PROPER CUSTARD

SERVES 4-6

250ml whole milk
250ml double cream
1 vanilla pod, split,
    or 1 tsp vanilla extract
1 coffee bean (optional)
6 egg yolks
50g caster sugar

Put the milk and cream in a pan with the vanilla pod or extract and the coffee bean, if using (it adds depth of flavour but doesn't make the custard taste of coffee). Bring the milk and cream almost to the boil, then remove the pan from the heat and set it aside for the flavours to infuse while the mixture cools.

Whisk the egg yolks and sugar together in a bowl until pale and foamy. Reheat the milk and cream, again to just below boiling point. Strain the milk mixture through a sieve into a jug and rinse out the saucepan. Slowly pour the milk mixture over the eggs, whisking constantly as you do so, then pour it all back into the saucepan. Set the pan over a very low heat and stir constantly until the custard has thickened slightly and you can draw a line through it when it coats the back of a spoon.

Strain the custard again and if you aren't serving it immediately, put the vanilla pod, if using, back into it. Cover the custard with cling film, making sure it comes into contact with the surface to prevent a skin from forming. Leave to cool.

VANILLA ICE CREAM

SERVES 4-6

300ml whole milk
300ml double cream
2 vanilla pods, split,
   or 2 tsp vanilla extract
4 egg yolks
100g caster sugar

Put the milk and the cream in a saucepan with the vanilla pods or extract. Bring it almost to the boil, then remove the pan from the heat and set it aside for the flavours to infuse while the mixture cools.

Have a bowl of ice-cold water ready to chill the custard down once you are happy with the thickness. Whisk the egg yolks and sugar together in a bowl until pale and foamy. Reheat the milk and cream, again until just below boiling point. Strain the milk mixture through a sieve into a jug and rinse out the saucepan. Slowly pour the milk mixture over the eggs, whisking constantly as you do so, then pour it all back into the saucepan. Set the pan over a very low heat and stir constantly until the custard has thickened slightly and you can draw a line through it when it coats the back of a spoon.

Plunge the pan into the bowl of ice-cold water to stop the custard cooking. Cover the custard with cling film to stop a skin forming, making sure the cling film touches the surface of the custard, then chill.

If you have an ice-cream maker, churn your ice cream, then transfer it to a container. If you don't have a machine, pile the mixture into a plastic container and freeze it immediately. Remove and whisk it vigorously every half an hour until it has completely set. Fifteen minutes before you want to serve the ice cream, take it out of the freezer and transfer it to the fridge.

INDEX

A

B

C

tomatoes

Cauliflower and quinoa bake 196

Chicken braised with bacon, red
wine and tomatoes 120

Chicken handi 96

Chilli con carne with corn
topping 172

Dal 272

Lamb and aubergine
casserole 140

Merguez sausages with
three-root mash 136

Mexican chicken with nachos 108

Pinto bean casserole 194

Pizza pie 186

Pot-roast chicken with pasta 100

Roast tomato and tuna
linguine 42

Shepherd's pie with couscous
topping 162

Tomato salsa 266

Tomato sauce 38, 50

Tortellini in brodo 24

tortillas

Fish finger fajitas 84

Margarita chicken fajitas 114

Veggie chilli burritos 190

Tray bake Christmas dinner 102

Trifle, Bakewell 216

tuna

Roast tomato and tuna
linguine 42

Tuna pasta bake 44

Vanilla ice cream 275

vegetables, mixed

Corned beef pasties 166

Fish and chorizo tray bake 78

Vegetable stock 256

Veggie chilli burritos 190

Veggie Scotch broth 20

see also soups

Vegetarian cottage pie 198–9

Victoria sponge 230

Vindaloo spice paste 259

walnuts

Chicken fesenjan 118

Coffee, walnut and date
cookies 242

Wild rice 262

Yoghurt dressing 182

Yorkshire pudding batter 132

THANK YOU LOVELY PEOPLE

As we explained in our introduction on pages 6-9, when we were planning this book we went on social media and asked you about your favourite things to eat. We promised to pick 100 names at random from the thousands who replied and publish them as a little thank you. So here are the lucky ones.

Marie Aubin	Jordan Denning	Alison Heather
Jennifer Baker	Nina Dominguez	Kylie Hilson
Lisa Bedder	Bettina Douglas	Karen Hilton
Zahra Bhatti	Karl Dransfield	Claire Holland
Sarah Bristow	Shaheen Dulloo	Serena Janssen
Denise Brooke	Andrew Eagle	Jack Jennings
Andrena Burns	Helen Fielding	Sarah Jevons
Amelia Chapman	Deborah Foley	Cate Johnson
Jen Charlton	Becky Forsythe	Sian Jones
Jacqui Clemson-Heath	Lauren Gardiner	Tracy Keane
Cathy Collins	Hannah Gibbs	Adam Khan
Adele Corry	Jack Goodman	Odette Krijthe
Ann Coyne	Jane Gregory	Brigitte Kuipers
Iona Crawford	Nancy Griffiths	Dawne Laing
Emma Dale	Keith Hallworth	Helen Larkin
Richard Dallaway	Roberta Hannon	Paula Lightfoot
Kelvin Davies	Hayley Hard	Adrian Lings

Paul Lyons

Stacey Machin

Nadine May

Laura McLaughlin

Valerie McNeish

William Mearns

Krystina Miles

Christy Lee Millar

John Miller

Judith Miller

Flavia Monni

Stacy Morrison

Veronica Morrison

Susan Murphy

Mark Osborn

Jacek Paszkowski

Juwairriyya Patel

Kim Pelling

John Philpott

Jennifer Piggin

Leila Reyhani

Aled Rhys-Jones

Simon Richards

Julie Roberts

Claire Robinson

Susan Rowledge

Erik Schoenmakers

Ian Sharp

Sharon Shulver

Sally Ann Smith

Brian Smyth

Martjin Spit

Tracey Stacey

Frances Stapleton

Lois Stevenson

Simone Struggles

Samantha Teun

Kate Tomkinson

Sue Tym

Andy Vickers

Ross Walton-Dalzell

Christopher Welch

Gina Willcocks

Emz Williams

Deborah Williamson

Tracy Willmers

Bradley Wills

Laura Wilson

Solat Zaidi

IT'S SILVER!

Believe it or not, this is the 25th book we've made together, so it's our silver anniversary! We would like to say the most massive thank you ever to all the people who've worked with us on these books over the years. You're an amazing bunch and we love you all.

We're really thrilled with this latest collection of recipes and we think our photographer, Andrew Hayes-Watkins, and the wonderful Mima Sinclair, food stylist, have outdone themselves and produced pictures that leap off the page and make our mouths water. Mima was ably assisted by Jemima O'Lone and Charlotte Whatcott and they all worked their socks off. As always, Tamzin Ferdinando came up with a fab selection of dishes and pans to make everything look its best.

Catherine Phipps is a true genius and works tirelessly to help us turn our ideas into the most sensational recipes. We love and admire you, Catherine.

The mega-talented designer, Lucie Stericker, and editor Jinny Johnson have both been with us since very early in our publishing career and we can't thank you both enough for all you have contributed. And thanks again to Elise See Tai for proofreading and Vicki Robinson for the index.

At Orion, our publisher Vicky Eribo kept us on track and gave us really great support and encouragement. And thank you too to Virginia Woolstencroft, head of publicity, for her input and to Nicole Abel for overseeing the production process. Also thanks to Alainna Hadjigeorgiou in publicity and to Lynsey Sutherland and Helena Fouracre in marketing.

And last but certainly not least, big thanks to Amanda Harris, our fabulous agent, friend and mentor, and to Emily Arthur and Elise Middleton at YMU.

We'd like to dedicate this book to all those people who took the time and trouble to fill in our survey. You've helped us make an amazing collection of recipes and for that we thank you.

First published in Great Britain in 2021 by Seven Dials
an imprint of The Orion Publishing Group Ltd
Carmelite House, 50 Victoria Embankment
London EC4Y 0DZ

An Hachette UK Company

1 3 5 7 9 10 8 6 4 2

A CIP catalogue record for this book is
available from the British Library.

ISBN (Hardback) 978 1 8418 8431 8
ISBN (eBook) 978 1 8418 8432 5

Publisher: Vicky Eribo
Recipe consultant: Catherine Phipps
Photography and styling: Andrew Hayes-Watkins
Design, illustration and art direction: Lucie Stericker, studio:715
Editor: Jinny Johnson
Food stylist: Mima Sinclair
Food stylist's assistants: Jemima O'Lone, Charlotte Whatcott
Prop stylist: Tamzin Ferdinando
Proofreader: Elise See Tai
Indexer: Vicki Robinson
Production manager: Nicole Abel

Printed in Germany